This is an inspiring series of reflections that flash through the mind in the course of daily affairs at this threatening moment in the history of the Earth.

—Thomas Berry, author *The Dream of the Earth*

Jim Conlon set himself an awesome task — to take the ordinary of daily life, reflect deeply on it, share his rich insights and, as if that were not enough, suggest many creative ways each of his readers could engage in the same process. What a gift! Many people awakening to a new Earth consciousness and looking for practices to ground their lives will welcome this book.

—Jane Blewett, Earth Community Center

If thoughtful people are right when they claim that society is following a law it no longer controls and that resists the efforts of social change, we are indeed standing on a precipice. Jim Conlon ponders the future with the belief that there are voices in the depth that call us to reconciliation with God, nature and other human beings.

—Gregory Baum, author *Man Becoming — God in Secular Experience*

If you are thinking that you have had just one too many books that have **soul** *in the title, restrain yourself from putting this book down. James Conlon's* **Ponderings from the Precipice: Soulwork for the New Millennium** *is a treasure of a book. Conlon situates his* **soulwork** *in the broadest context, that is, what Brian Swimme and Thomas Berry call* **The Universe Story**. *Conlon's work situates the universe context within a deeply held context of both social justice and earth justice. The word* **ponderings** *in the title lets the reader know that this is a book of reflection and, specifically, a book on self-reflection for people who consciously cultivate and nourish their spiritual life at the millennial turning point. James Conlon gives his reader an incredible variety of reflections that are important seeds for their contemplative life. He provides a feast of beautiful quotes that the reader can savor. The author brings to the reader a Christian context, but a non-Christian reader can also get much soul food in his ponderings. A work of great generosity and depth.*

—Edmund O'Sullivan, director, Transformative Learning Center; author *The Dream Drives the Action*

Jim Conlon is a valued colleague and friend who is one of the finest teachers of earth-based spirituality that I know.

—Tom Hayden, California Senator, author *Lost Gospel of the Earth*

*Jim Conlon's **Ponderings from the Precipice: Soulwork for the New Millennium** is about much more than changing our calendars or computer clocks! It is, as John Shea says in the Preface, about moving from what is dying into what is coming to birth in individuals, in communities and in Earth's community.*

*   **Ponderings** is a user's manual for travelers on this journey. It is a questioner's workbook that nourishes mind and soul. Organized around life's recurring themes of Rediscovering Fire, Shattering, An Integral Life, and Beginning Again, the book is a treasure of practical wisdom. Short reflections and "soulwork" of suggested actions or questions weave personal story and historical events into a framework that supports authentic human living and sound ecological citizenship.*

*   Themes, and often sentences, break open extraordinary events like letter writing, birthdays, cultural violence, singing the song of nature, energy for justice making, and transitions. Side-bar quotes and Projects for an Ecological Age provide powerful soul food. **Ponderings** is a wonderful guide for entering the next millennium, the Ecological Era.*

—Mary Lou Dolan, Earth Literacy Program, St. Mary's-of-the-
      Woods College

If we only had this book to guide our thinking and actions years ago, it would have helped us to think differently about God's magnificent creation and the relationship of each person to the other and together for the world that God has entrusted to us.

*   This is a prophetic book, one which should be read by every person who loves life and dreams about our evolving as free persons and our future.*

*   I would heartily recommend the reading of **Ponderings from the Precipice** by every responsible person who is looking forward to a new era where our relationships with each other will bring about the liberation of both humanity and Earth.*

—Msgr. John J. Egan, DePaul University

Ponderings

from the

Precipice

Soulwork for the New Millennium

James Conlon

FOREST OF PEACE
Publishing

Suppliers for the Spiritual Pilgrim
Leavenworth, KS

Ponderings from the Precipice

copyright © 1998, by James Conlon

Library of Congress Cataloging-in-Publication Data

Conlon, James, 1936-
  Ponderings from the precipice : soulwork for the new millennium /
    James Conlon.
      p.   cm.
  ISBN 0-939516-40-3
  1. Meditations.   I. Title.
BX2182.2.C66   1998
242—dc21   98-6246
                                                   CIP

published by

Forest of Peace Publishing, Inc.
PO Box 269
Leavenworth, KS 66048-0269   USA
1-800-659-3227

printed by

Hall Directory, Inc.
Topeka, KS 66608-0007

1st printing: March 1998

Dedication

Other times in history
Thought they were it
They were wrong
This is it.

—Jean Houston

Our time is now.

—Christopher Fry

Inside me dwells two million stars
One for each of my ancestors.

—Nancy Wood

To the Galaxies and Earth and all whose lives have come before.

To my Irish and French ancestors of yesterday and today, whose courage and adventurous spirit brought them to Canada from far off.

To my family of today, particularly my brother, Bob, and my sister, Mary, with whom I share a common story and the continuity of family roots.

To each of the authors and activitists whose words appear in these pages and whose wisdom and vision point us toward the future.

To all the children, whose lives are here at the precipice.

And to the yet-unborn of every species, whose lives will begin tomorrow and whose legacy is the new millennium.

Acknowledgments

To Thomas Skorupa of Forest of Peace Publishing, whose commitment to this project and good work helped make this book possible.

To Joan LaFlamme, whose editorial talent has touched every page.

To Marilyn Goddard, Connie Krautkramer, Cathryn Farrell and Katherine Osburn, whose generosity and work have contributed greatly to the birth of this book.

May the present bring joy
Yesterday, gratitude
And tomorrow, hope.

Tell me, what is it you plan to do
With your one wild and precious life?

—Mary Oliver

There is in all things an invisible fecundity
A dimmed life
A meek namelessness
A hidden wholeness.

—Thomas Merton

One way to open your eyes to unnoticed beauty
is to ask yourself:
What if I had never seen this before?
What if I knew I would never see it again?

—Rachel Carson

Contents

Preface:

The Path of Precipice Pondering

I believe it was F. Scott Fitzgerald who said, "Draw your chair up close to the precipice and I'll tell you a story."

Jim Conlon issues the same invitation. He wants to tell us a story of what is dying and what is coming to birth. This is a tale of dizzying heights and steep plunges, a tale best told from a precipice.

There is a price to be paid in accepting this invitation and listening to this story. In the Christian Gospels the King sends out an invitation to the great feast. But people have other things to do. The pressing affairs of everyday life keep them from attending. "I have bought a piece of land . . . I have bought five yoke of oxen . . . I have been married . . . ." There are land deals, cattle purchases and relationships to keep us occupied. In other words, the invitation is in competition with business as usual.

Jim Conlon's invitation is particularly threatening to business as usual. He believes a new era is upon us. If we do not work with it, we may be in the unenviable position that Einstein predicted: "Everything has changed except our thinking." It is our thinking that needs changing. More fundamentally, it is our consciousness that needs to be restructured.

So the chair on the precipice is a seat of pondering. The pondering is not merely a process of mental consideration. The pondering entails soulwork — exercises and suggestions that lead to integrating the insights of the pondering. This is a book of high spiritual expectation. It wants inner transformation to eventuate in different and more congruent outer actions. Pick it up at your own risk.

The primary spiritual texts of my life are the Christian Gospels. So when I read Jim's invitation, I think of the path of pondering that is present in Luke's Gospel. Luke also thought a new world was upon the people of his day. They had to appropriate this newness at great depth or they would be paralyzed by the past or swept away by the future. So he proposed a model of how to ponder on the crucial events that were happening. The model's name was Mary.

The best way to understand the nature of pondering is to see it as a middle option between dismissal and amazement. In Luke's infancy narrative, Zachary is the figure of dismissal, and the people who hear about the birth of Christ are figures of amazement. Between them is the woman who has learned the art of "pondering in her heart."

In Luke's story the angel Gabriel appears to both Zachary and Mary. When he appears to the aged Zachary and tells him that he is soon to be a father, Zachary responds, "How shall I know this? For I am an old man and my wife is advanced in years." Gabriel is not happy with this response. He reminds Zachary, "I am Gabriel who stands in the presence of God. I was sent to speak to you and bring you this good news." Free paraphrase: "Let's get things straight. I represent the power of God, and I'm on mission to tell you what God is doing. And your only reaction is to doubt that it can happen?" Zachary is then silenced until the birth he did not think could happen has come about. This silence will give him time to do what he did not do. He will have the needed time to ponder.

When Gabriel appears to Mary, he greets her, "Hail, O highly favored one! The Lord is with you." Her response to this salutation is to be troubled. These words are foreign to her. But she does not immediately question them. "She considered in her mind what this greeting might mean." Mary is a ponderer of what she does not immediately understand. Zachary's doubt effectively dismisses the angel's message. Mary entertains his troublesome words, troublesome because they do not easily fit into Mary's way of thinking. By the time she asks her question, "How can this be, since I do not know man?" it is not to doubt the message but to figure out what she must do to cooperate with it. She is trying to integrate the higher wisdom of the angel into her existing categories. Even further, she is inquiring about how to enact the word she is hearing. She is into "soulwork." The proper response to higher wisdom is pondering what you are only beginning to understand.

Luke stresses this pondering activity of Mary. When the shepherds make known what the angel told them and how they found the child, "all who heard it were amazed." But not Mary. "She kept all these things, pondering them in her heart." After the episode of losing and finding the boy Jesus in the Temple, Luke again tells us that "his mother pondered these things in her heart." Mary lives between the dismissal of Zachary and the amazement of the crowds. She is, in essence, a ponderer.

This, I think, is a clue to how to receive Jim Conlon's invitation. Do not play Zachary and dismiss it out of hand because it does not fit with your conventional categories. Do not play the shepherds and be mindlessly amazed by it. Play Mary and take it into your heart and ponder it.

Later in the Gospel, Luke further explores this idea of pondering. In Jesus' explanation of the parable of the sower, the good soil that yields a hundred fold are those "who, hearing the word, hold it fast in an honest and good heart, and bring forth fruit in patience" (Luke 8: 15). To me this describes the process of pondering and soulwork that Jim suggests. "Holding it fast" points to the difficulty of turning a fleeting insight into a steady form of seeing. It is one thing to have a moment of illumination; it is quite another thing to see persistently from a spiritual point of view. Pondering may produce insights, but insights fade fast. They need to be secured.

This "ongoing holding" has to be done in an "honest and good heart." The heart is the deepest center of the person. It is the soul space that is the core of spiritual consciousness, that space that in the back (so to speak) opens into the infinite world of spirit and in the front (so to speak) flows in mind and body and out into the world. This space is a place of both honesty and goodness. The thousand ways we deceive ourselves have to be recognized and released. There has to be an acknowledgment of the truth of the human condition. The foolishness of clinging to perishing forms of physical and social life must be confronted with clear eyes. This honest appraisal is the prerequisite for goodness. The good heart enacts the wisdom it is beginning to understand. The good follows the true.

But the producing of this good fruit will take place in patience. Spiritual transformation from the center of the self to the circumference, from the depth to the surface, from the inside to the outside, is not cosmetic change. It is the integration of spiritual wisdom into a conflicted mind and knotted body, and then through a series of endless experiments into a world of faithfulness and deceit.

This seems to me what Jim Conlon is inviting us to do. This is a book of spiritual exercises. Jim says they are "intended as a companion for moments of meditation woven into the many demands of the modern day." He nicknames this book "subway reading."

Don't be surprised if you miss your stop.

John Shea

Proclamation of Trust

I believe in the gospel of life.
I believe that it touches every aspect of our lives.
I believe that the divine presence permeates every moment and place
     of our existence.
I believe that all of life is sacred and sacramental.
I believe we are summoned by the gospel to a life of peace, prayer,
     compassion and justice-making.
I believe the call to work for the transformation of society and Earth
     is a special gift,
an invitation to participate in building the kingdom of God on this
     fragile planet.
I believe that what we most profoundly desire and know as just and true
     is rooted in the Gospel of tradition and the natural world.
I believe that if we keep our hearts and minds open to the
     beauty and the crises of our time
we will make connections between our deepest convictions
     and what we are called to do.

—Jim Conlon

To believe in God is to build a bridge between yourself and everything
worth being one with.

—Corita Kent

This story calls us to deepen our understanding of life's self-organizing
processes and of our own conscious intelligence, and to master the art of
living . . . to give birth to a culture that values sufficiency, cooperation,
love and stewardship; to create self-regulating, non-hierarchical
organizations that liberate and celebrate our higher potentials.

—David Korten

We ourselves feel what we are doing is just a drop in the ocean,
but if that drop were not in the ocean, I think the ocean would be less
because of that missing drop.

—Mother Teresa

12

PROLOGUE:
Pondering at the Precipice

This is an idea whose time has come.... The world will not survive the 21st century with the ethics of the 20th century.

—Dr. Oscar Arias, Nobel Prize winner
and former leader of Costa Rica

The damaged Earth, violent and unjust social structures, the lonely and broken heart —all cry out for a fresh start.

—Elizabeth Johnson

We Begin with a Story

It was Easter Sunday in South Carolina. We were on our way to the airport at Myrtle Beach to fly back to San Francisco. The landscape announced the coming of spring on that Easter day. Flowers were bursting into bloom, the birds were celebrating the season, while behind the wheel Helen was telling her story.

As the highway stretched out before us, she recalled her work with abandoned children. She remembered staying up all night with Michael, not knowing whether he would live through the night. She told us with great joy of his recovery and adoption. While happy for his health, she recalled how her heart was broken when the funding for the project ran out.

Helen often spent her free time visiting people in prison. She mused about the Sunday afternoon she had visited John in a Kentucky prison. As she approached the visiting area, she saw that John had gashes on his wrists; his clothes were tousled and he was emotionally distraught. Gazing at his wrists, he said, "As soon as you leave, I'm going to finish the job."

Helen reminded John of his beautiful young daughter, whom he loved very much. A few moments later the guard announced it would soon be time to leave. As they were about to part, Helen spoke to John: "I'll be here tomorrow. If you're alive, we'll visit. If you're dead, I'll pray for you."

Moved by her declaration and her understanding, John reached down into the cuff of his pants and retrieved a piece of jagged glass. As he handed it to Helen, he said, "I'll see you tomorrow."

This story is indeed a pondering from a precipice; it is archetypal and symbolic for our time. John, in prison, represents not only each individual but a culture and planet on the precipice of destruction and danger here at the doorway of the twenty-first century. Choruses of prophets of doom and events like the Oklahoma City bombing, the inferno at Waco, Texas, and the mass suicide of the Heaven's Gate group cause the specter of Armageddon and the End Times to hang in the air about us.

Sitting at the precipice is a time to recollect. This period of planetary crisis and transition is a time for each of us to get back to our roots, to return to the source stories that have shaped our sense of the sacred. As we reflect on the sacred stories of our tradition and the story of the universe, we find a ground of hope. We realize that we are deeply connected to each other, to all that is and to the Divine Source. As we reflect on our own stories and recall periods of personal transition — even when they are experienced as times of painful crisis, of closing down or impasse — we recognize the divine activity in the turning points of our lives. As we extract the significance of our personal stories, we discover the precipice as a moment of paradox. At the precipice we feel the pain of people with broken hearts and broken dreams, the profound sense of homelessness, fractured relationships and a wounded ecosystem; at the same time, it is a place of promise, possibility, passion and compassion. It is potentially a place of creativity and new beginnings. As we uncover our deeper identities disclosed in our stories, wider possibilities unfold and dreams emerge from our depths, bringing us closer to God's dream for us, the dream of a planetary Pentecost. We realize that each of our stories is archetypal, recognizing in them the patterns of the primal sacred stories, recognizing in them the footprints of God. Each of us is challenged during these dark and dangerous times to say to each other and to our planet, "I'll see you tomorrow." We are challenged to sound a clarion call of hope.

It is in this spirit of story as pattern and teacher that I relate some of my own story, encouraging you to recollect, listen to and tell your own.

Where It Began

My name is Jim Conlon. My father was Irish. He traced his origins back to Ireland where in 1843 his great-grandparents left their home in South Armaugh and set sail for Canada. My mother was French-Canadian. Her ancestors left France in 1658 and set out for Canada from Rochelle. As a

14

child I lived with my parents, brother and sister in Sombra (population 300), a village in southwestern Ontario. We attended St. John's Catholic Church on Sundays. The church was a rural mission with no resident priest. Apart from an occasional catechetical program in the summer, I received no religious instruction. Yet in my family and community, faith was important. My father never missed a funeral; local weddings were community festivals. I was taught that the sacraments were important benchmarks for our lives. Even as a child I came to recognize that significant transitions were marked by sacramental celebrations of weddings, baptisms, anointings and funerals. Family prayer, most often the Rosary, was a daily event. The ethos of faith and the Christian tradition had a profound impact on my life.

A Broader World

The first step that took me out of my hometown occurred when I attended Assumption University of Windsor in Ontario, Canada. I studied chemistry and graduated with a bachelor of science degree. Along the way I took courses in theology — actually, basic catechetics. Many of my classmates had studied this material in elementary and high school. But it was a very different experience for me. I was hearing it all for the first time.

After graduation I enrolled in St. Peter's Seminary in London, Ontario. This was before the Vatican Council II. The theology we were taught was very much the result of the Council of Trent, the council that had been convoked after the Protestant Reformation. As I reflect back, I can say that the mood was apologetic. Orthodoxy and denominational identity were high on the agenda. Ecumenism, dialogue and respect for world religions were not seen as important — and perhaps were even viewed with suspicion. Even though Vatican II took place while I was in the seminary, it was out of a pre–Vatican II background and education that I was ordained.

Yet ordination was a significant day for me. It was accompanied by a rainbow of emotions, ranging from gratitude to terror. Perhaps the dominant one was fear — uncertainty about the future and the implications of commitment. I was aware that our lives unfold inextricably into the future.

Post–Vatican II

The days after my ordination and the impact of Vatican II dramatically influenced my life. Pope John XXIII had opened the windows of the church and given us a new vision. Yet my education and background in rural Ontario had not prepared me well for the rapid changes that were soon to break into the consciousness of the culture.

Vatican II theology, particularly the *Church in the Modern World* document, changed my perspective on the meaning of being a Christian. I began to realize that religion, faith and justice were not confined to denomination or place. Now an associate pastor, I began to reach out to and develop programs with other Christian groups and with the wider community. The Christian Family Movement, for example, became an interdenominational project based on "living room dialogues" with members from Protestant churches and Jewish synagogues.

The parish was replaced by the community as the context for being a Christian. Other people of good will were no longer "anonymous Christians"; they were people whose faith and spiritual journeys were authentic and significant. I discovered a new world of ecumenical colleagues. These were people who shared a common experience of the divine and a common passion for justice.

This new involvement resulted in my gaining permission to study urban training and community organization in Toronto and Chicago.

Organizing

I had not yet read Meister Eckhart's statement, "If you understand what I have to say about justice, you will understand everything I have to say." However, I had come to understand the concept and believe it.

As I moved away from the parish as a base and into the community as an organizer, I became aware that liberation and justice-making were at the center of my operative theology. After studying at the Canadian Urban Training Project for Christian Service in Toronto, I moved to Chicago with the counsel and advice of Msgr. Jack Egan, then at the University of Notre Dame. In Chicago I was to meet Saul Alinsky, Jim Morton, Marjorie Tuite, O.P., Gino Baroni, and many others engaged in the justice agenda of the American church. This experience radicalized my politics and transformed my experience of the Gospel. As I wrote to a friend:

> I find this stuff so exciting. It seems for years I've been working through and with structures that militate against liberating people and serving them. The whole thing that turns me on about community organization is that it provides a vehicle whereby most people can move and struggle out of their own passions and interest in life. I feel that this kind of work is very much connected with the Gospel and the kind of ministry I feel more and more inclined to practice and learn about.

In Pursuit of Self-Discovery

I began the pursuit of self-discovery in 1968; it was only later that I comprehended the significance of that act. With the convening of Vatican II and the events that followed, I and so many others hoped that our fondest dreams for the future of church and society would be fulfilled. We dreamed of a democratized church, a socially just society and a political system based on leadership, equality and courage. We longed for a spirituality that might touch our lives, encourage us in our struggles and name our deepest experiences of the divine. Yet 1968 was a watershed moment that confronted us with the sobering awareness that our hopes would not be realized. When *Humane Vitae* was published, it marked the closing down of the energies evoked by John XXIII. Bobby Kennedy was assassinated in Los Angeles, and the Democratic Convention declared the bankruptcy of the political system. When Martin Luther King, Jr., was felled by a bullet in Memphis, the Civil Rights Movement went awry. Thomas Merton was electrocuted in Bancock; Daniel and Philip Berrigan were members of the Cantonville Nine protesting the Viet Nam War; the Immaculate Heart Sisters of Los Angeles found themselves on a collision course with church authorities over differing approaches to renewal. Earth was seen for the first time from out in space. On some level not yet conscious I realized the structures would not change. I had to change myself. I entered therapy.

Changes occurred in rapid order; these changes in lifestyle, world view, work and belief systems had a profound emotional impact on my life. I felt a need to learn and understand more about myself. It was in therapy that trust, hope, death, love and compassion became more than categories of thought. They became more integral and understood; these were the things now central to my existence. Although I had read and studied about the relationship of psychology and religion, now I felt I was beginning to understand these formerly academic ideas from the perspective of my own experience. I asked myself what being in therapy said about my being a priest. I felt both stimulated by and afraid of this new process I had begun.

One important insight for me was that upset does not necessarily point toward pathology. It may be an impulse toward greater balance. Problems and pain may be sources of wholeness and healing.

Beyond Psychology to Ecology

A significant shift in my spiritual journey was my introduction to *ecological theology*. I began to expand my horizons from the human to the entire earth community. My life was shaken to its foundations. The language of Pierre Teilhard de Chardin named my experience: a *shattering* of my worldview was taking place.

In July, 1983, I participated in a workshop of the Institute in Cultural and Creation Spirituality (ICCS) and the following year responded to an invitation to take my sabbatical with ICCS at Holy Names College in Oakland, California. During that first year at ICCS, my years of pastoral work, urban training, community organizing, psychotherapy, teaching and social-justice work all came under intense self-scrutiny. My world view was changing — and so was everything else! I was questioning all the time: What was work? justice? belief? Just what was my relationship to creation? to myself? to others?

I began to think about my study of chemistry, my years of working in the Imperial Oil Laboratories in Canada's "chemical valley." I realized that I — and my community — had been engaged in the struggle for technological dominance. My life, and the lives of my family and friends, had been caught up in the struggle to "get back to bliss" by using technology to overcome the obstacles that kept us from "the garden" — often at the expense of the natural world.

Out of that year of reflection, and the years that have followed, I have come to understand three aspects that have significantly affected my commitment and my belief:

1. I experienced that the divine is present in all of life. I understood that *everything* is sacred and sacramental. My understandings were stretched beyond the human to embrace all creation. Through a theology of panentheism I discovered that God is in all things and all things are in God. The categories of church, justice and revelation called out for a new understanding. The sacredness of existence had permeated my consciousness and dramatically altered my understanding.

2. I began to understand that the universe is developing and is interconnected by origin. I began to appreciate that the transformative events that name the origin and evolution of the universe — and the human — are sacred and revelatory. As a child, college student and seminarian, I had learned the Genesis story of a world created by God and redeemed by the Incarnate Son. Scripture, research and form criticism had revealed more about the Christian story; I knew that it was revelatory and the source of our belief and tradition. I also understood that it was not to be taken as a scientific account but as a mythic context for our lives and as a historical plan of salvation. Over the years I have come to realize that what creation spirituality calls the *New Story* does not contradict or replace the Genesis story; rather, it complements it and gives it a new and more powerful meaning.

3. The revelation communicated to us by the divine through the New Story is not limited to words but comes through images and perception. With new eyes we awaken to that communication spoken through meadow, brook, bird, tree and human. I am now free to focus more on divine creation than redemption; to see humans as new arrivals on the planet; to feel embraced by and connected to all of life. The story of humanity is a paragraph in the great New Story of the universe — if the history of the universe were projected onto a one-year time line, the history of humanity would occupy only the final ten minutes of December 31. I believe in the sacredness of all of life and believe that all creation has a spiritual and sacred dimension. The New Story is one of reverence and awe.

I have been tremendously influenced by this most recent spiritual transition. Now all those things that matter so deeply — justice, faith, integrity, the experience of the divine — come together. I've tried to express this in a poem:

A Canticle for Geo-Justice

Where there are ruptures in divine creation,
We are aroused to peace.

Where there is disquietude,
We are invited to balance.

Where there is discord,
We are attuned to resonance.

In and through the pain of our wounded planet
We are called to make our Easter with the Earth.

From collapse and devastation
We rediscover within the risen heart of the universe:

Cosmic peace
Profound harmony
Deep balance
Compassionate resonance
Pentecost for the Earth and
Geo-Justice with the universe.

Although I have felt I was called to "make [my] Easter with the Earth," I sensed there was more to come. Easter was followed by Pentecost, the arrival of the Spirit. How am I to know the Spirit? How do I aid in the work of the Spirit? What are the signs of the Spirit's presence among us? This is what I believe:

A Planetary Pentecost

A planetary Pentecost happens through relationship and interconnectedness
  when all creation experiences harmony, balance and peace;
  when each member of the Earth community engages in reciprocal actions
    that prompt transformation and peace;
  when the creative energy of the divine permeates the natural world and
    elevates all creation to an expression of sacredness and grace;
  when the unfolding story of the universe focuses our journey and
    animates the landscape of our soul;
  when we discover who we are, whence we've come and
    where we're going;
  when the original "fireball" erupts in our psyches and is revealed
    in the events of our day.

This is what I believe — and this is who I am. I have come to see and understand the challenge for each of us to participate in the dynamic integration of two narrations: the Story of the Universe that is emerging into our consciousness and the Story of Geo-Justice that finds its source in the sacred impulse to live out a preferential option for Earth and every species.

As we envision the possibilities for the future, we also strive to grasp the crisis of our moment and explore the options that lie ahead.

As an Era Ends

Cultural historian Thomas Berry points out that we are positioned at the end of an era. We have basically four options:

- ◆ We can have a tantrum and collapse.
- ◆ We can jump off the precipice and end our lives.
- ◆ We can continue living just as we have been — either out of personal integrity or because we fail to grasp the severity of the situation.
- ◆ We can turn around, march away from the precipice, begin again and keep going until the planetary Pentecost becomes present in our midst.

Ponderings from the Precipice is an invitation to take the last alternative, to move into a world of relationship, inclusion and change as we attempt to live fully and with a passionate responsibility for the Earth and every species.

Our quest is about justice: for humans, but also for rocks, waters and trees and all other creatures. We celebrate the pursuit of a Geo-Justice, which announces that the experience of the poor and the poor Earth are both domains of the divine activity and that they contain a blueprint of freedom for tomorrow.

In relationship with the poor and poor Earth, we look for the courage necessary to move us forward into a hope-filled yet fragile future which holds the promise of clean water, clean air and toward a culture that is committed to equality, honors difference, celebrates depth and promotes connectedness.

The New Story — The Universe Story

As a child, and now as an adult, I have often wondered why my world felt static and fixed. The message I received is that the universe and Earth were placed here. Everything was constant and eternal — and, by implication, unchangeable. As a Christian, I saw God as constant and unchanging too. Everything was like that: eternal and fixed. It was from this perspective that I began to examine evolution and its implication for our lives.

When I heard that Edwin Hubbell saw from his telescope that the universe was *expanding*, everything changed. We had learned something very new. When we go beyond this empirical data and see the events of an expanding universe as sacred and revelatory, we have discovered the meaning of the universe's story. When we realize that the events of the galactic period, the Earth period, the life on Earth period and the human period are revelatory, we have discovered what Thomas Aquinas called "the book of the natural world." This New Story complements the book of Scripture as a source of revelation, and with these two sources we gain perspective on our ponderings from the precipice. We see that all life is revelatory and that it unfolds. We realize that tomorrow will be different than today. We discover that we are being thrust into an uncertain and exciting future. Suddenly, our world of "fixed truths and unchanging doctrines" is challenged. The New Story teaches us to accept new revelations and to integrate them into a transforming spirituality. In its wake, everything becomes sacred and revelatory. We are challenged to celebrate diversity, interconnectedness and depth as we look forward to the possibility and promise that envelops and energizes our lives.

A Clarion Call — Reaching for Reciprocity

Movements represent the principle of flux and change: they are the processes through which a society channels its renewal and transformation.

—Parker Palmer

I believe that we live in a time that must dare to call for and begin to build a movement, a movement that will heal our souls and the soul of a culture in need of new vision, new energy and a renewed sense of hope.

We need to speak the words of movement again to a country and a constituency that is hungry for justice and longs for peace. For me, to build a movement is a fantastic adventure, a call to live at ability's edge, to gather as friends and sometimes even to smile through struggle, celebration and tears.

To build a movement will take imagination and courage. It cannot be learned in a classroom or read out of a book. It is, and will be, written and transcribed in the lives of people like you who struggle for passion and purpose to build relationships and reciprocity and peace. Each of us will get up every morning and put our hearts and our hopes on the line. We will each day face possible failure along with the hope that tomorrow can be better than today.

Our movement will be created by energy, courage and ideas, by constant effort and deep trust, by relationships and love that become the context of our lives. As we build this movement, our lives will be filled with creativity, wonder and delight. We will dissolve rigidity and separateness as we become vulnerable and rededicate ourselves to justice for a people and the planet as we once again remember our original purpose.

As we foster our movement, we will be reenergized by a high degree of consciousness, focus and cohesion. Our movement will be marked by relationships of reciprocity that reflect the dynamics of the universe. We will continue to celebrate our connectedness across gender, geography and race. We will honor our uniqueness, as well as come home to the diversity and difference expressed in a rainbow of many forms. As we reverence the inwardness and depths of each expression of creation and experience again a sense of the sacred, we will become the touchstone that holds us together in a compassionate embrace as we become a coalition for Earth and every species.

From this place our movement will find expression in the "quantum structures" of a coalition that is functional and fluid while focusing on a genetic task that is centered yet unfolding, liberating yet rooted.

It is a movement that celebrates our relationship to every species, that is guided by the Spirit of the compassionate dynamics of the universe and energized by the prophetic vision of Gandhi, King, Day and those who will follow, as well as those who have gone before. It is a movement marked by voluntary simplicity, whose participants' lives are marked by the imprints of sacrifice and sacredness. Only then will we be energized to stretch the boundaries of our comfort zones, to take action, search for common ground, remove stereotypes, become open to the depth of the challenge, make sure we have fun and see that spirituality is at the root and the source of the movement we are now called upon to build.

Prayer from the Precipice

It is from the perspective of the precipice that we hear the clarion call to renewal and transformation. From the precipice we realize that we are living in a culture of accelerating change, and it is clear that much that is happening is destructive. Economic systems produce winners and losers. Consumerism proliferates and results in the pollution of our spirit as well as our planet home. Political parties increasingly fail to represent us, and we increasingly ignore the voting booth and relinquish the leadership of our country and continent to the rule of transnational companies and corporate elites. Congregations "gray" and participation declines as religious institutions become further disconnected from the "people in the pew." Because we desire security in this uncertain world, fundamentalism is growing in its appeal and, for many people, displacing the open-minded quest for meaning and purpose so needed in all our lives.

Ponderings from the Precipice is one response to our turbulent times. It is an invitation to ponder key questions that confront us at this point in history. Each reflection is short, designed as "subway reading," intended as a companion for moments of meditation woven into the many demands of the modern day. Yet perhaps it is in just such brief but pregnant moments that we find grace and insight into the seemingly insoluble issues of this time of crisis and transition.

The *soulwork* section of each *pondering* offers concrete ways to explore these questions further and, more important, to carry the reflections into action for the individual, the community and the Earth.

Let's begin these ponderings with a meditation.

> God of Creation,
>> called forth by wisdom's crises,
>> we edge unknowingly
>> to the precipice of our era and time,
>> summoned by insight, intuition, and you.
>
> With grounded joy
>> we confront the options of our day
>> and collectively decide
>> to return and begin anew.
>
> At this moment of hindsight and apprehension,
>> this time of depth and healing,
>> we are called to reinvent our culture and ourselves
>> here on the precipice of new beginnings.

I.

Rediscovering Fire

I thought the Earth
remembered me . . . tenderly . . . . I slept . . .
between me and the white fire of the stars . . . .

—Mary Oliver, "Sleeping in the Forest"

The day will come after harnessing space
            the wind
            the tides
            and gravitation
We will harness for God the energies of love
And on that day for the second time in the history of the world
We shall have discovered fire.

—Teilhard de Chardin

            Where is your fire?
            You've got to find it
            And pass it on.

            Catch the fire and
            Burn with eyes
            That see our souls
                    Walking
                    Singing
                    Building
                    Learning
                    Loving
                    Teaching
            Catch the fire and live.

—Sonia Sanchez

The God of My Childhood

Pondering

As a child, I often wondered about God. My mother had told me that God is in church. I remember looking for "him" in that white frame building on the shore of the St. Clair River in rural Ontario. However much I tried, I felt unsatisfied with my search.

Each evening my father would lead us in the Rosary. It seemed we were praying to a God I didn't know. Without a clear description or understanding, I felt that God was distant, up in the sky. The phrase "God's in his heaven, all's right with the world" had somehow become ingrained in my consciousness.

It seemed that most of my friends and family were afraid of God. God was not only distant but the stern judge, the gatekeeper to heaven. I learned that an important goal in life was forgiveness; without forgiveness we would not go to heaven.

Because God was in heaven, it was important to get there. Thus we seemed to spend our time getting ready; life felt like a vestibule to heaven, a preparation to meet and appease a distant judge.

Somehow I sensed, even as a child, that things were out of balance, that something was not right. The God that we worshiped and feared was like an absentee landlord, yet we were supposed to love this God "with all our heart, soul, mind and strength," as the catechism put it. But the God of my childhood was not lovable, not even approachable.

Eventually I came to realize that the hunger, hope and even despair that hovered in my heart and consciousness were impulses in and toward the divine. And suddenly, or perhaps not so suddenly, things began to shift. My sense and experience of God, church and prayer were in transition. I learned that all life embodies the divine: the river, trees, children. The Earth is a place where God dwells. God, the distant resident of heaven, sometimes housed in churches, became the divine, an indwelling, permeating presence, a

Any time, day or night, at home or in the street, wherever we are, we live bathed in God.

—Dom Helder Camara

Why should I wish to see God better than this day?

I see something of God In each hour of the twenty-four.

In the face of men and women, I see God And in my own face in the glass.

—Walt Whitman

25

sacred envelope that embraced and made all life a sacrament. The barriers between yesterday, today and tomorrow collapsed. I prayed "thy kingdom come" with new hope and awareness.

Our thinking about God is indeed very important. Thomas Berry, geologian and cultural historian, would say we have had too much transcendence. He is suggesting that because we have viewed God as distant, we have lost sight of the sacredness and divine presence that permeates all existence. Because of this we have tended to mistreat the Earth and its people. We need to incorporate into our outlook a significant sense of the immanent presence of the divine. Mechtild of Magdeburg speaks of a healthy balance between immanence and transcendence: "On the day of my spiritual awakening, I saw and knew that I saw God in all things and all things in God."

Such healthy panentheism also implies what Meister Eckhart would call the Godhead or the *beyondness* of God. In our ponderings for the new millennium, I suggest that we can be nurtured by an awareness of the sacredness of life as well as the deep mystery of God who is both distant and inviting. For me, God has become a mysterious, approachable presence, and that presence is right in the middle of matter, right in the midst of life.

My prayer has become a "walkabout," a moving upon the Earth and celebrating each being as a manifestation of God. Church has become a circle of relationship.

> The sense of the Earth opening and exploding upward into God . . . and the sense of God taking root and finding nourishment, downward into Earth.
>
> —Teilhard de Chardin

Soulwork

The church's liturgical calendar marks the feast of the Annunciation, the day Mary was told that she was to be the mother of God. Twelve hundred years later Meister Eckhart would say from the pulpit of the Cologne Cathedral, "What difference does it make if the Christ child was born 1200 years ago if I do not give birth to the Son of God in my life?"

Listen to the various needs of the Earth today. What "annunciations" are being made in your life? How will you respond?

Prayer

Pondering

Prayer once puzzled me, particularly the prayer of petition. Is prayer a way to change God's mind? I wondered. I prayed for my mother when she had cancer, but she didn't get well. Was my prayer answered? Did God say no? My catechism said that prayer was "the elevation of the heart and mind to God." What did that mean?

Later I began to understand that prayer was more about gratitude and praise than "give me and forgive me." It was not about changing God but rather about the way in which I engaged in the process of life.

I now believe that prayer is largely about "conscious presence" — about paying attention to the divine, who is already here. In fact, prayer is less about words than about listening and responding. Prayer is about opening to the epiphany moments that come to us, that speak to us in every aspect of our lives and through all creation. Prayer is about engaging with God, who is living, affective, transforming — who is mystery. Prayer provides the energy we need to live our lives with depth, dedication, identity and purpose.

In prayer we involve ourselves in all that is. Prayer calls us to acknowledge our membership in the community of creation. It invites us to live reflectively with Earth. It is more about being than doing, more about presence than petition. Prayer is living our humanity with depth, spontaneity and compassion. Prayer is awakening to who we are; it is our story lived out each day.

Soulwork

The spirituality of "spending time with," of carefully "attending to," is an important practice, one that creates and strengthens relationships. The healing of fractured families and a wounded Earth requires nurturing a connection and weaving a tapestry of oneness. Today, try to dissolve the distance by spending time with those who matter to you.

"Have a good day!" What's behind this greeting? Is it

> I don't know what prayer is, but I do know how to pay attention.
>
> —Mary Oliver

> And now I think for the first time in my whole life I really began to pray — praying not with my lips and with my intellect and my imagination, but praying out of the very roots of my life and of my being and praying to the God I had never known . . . .
>
> —Thomas Merton

27

a wish that you will find meaning or purpose in your life? That you will stop long enough to enjoy moments of exchange and experiences of beauty? That you will profit from your accomplishments and network of relationships? Take the time to reflect on the depth and breadth of your existence, the *raison d'etre* of your being.

People who come together find that their relationships are altered by the melding of their separate stories into a common story. Allow your story to come alive again among those who share your history: your spouse, friends, brothers, sisters, parents, children. Take time today to remember and tell your personal and family stories, and remember to tell the common source stories — including the story of the universe.

Take time to share your stories in an attitude of paying attention to the universe and our place in it, a posture of prayer.

Prayer is nothing but the inhaling and exhaling of the one breath of the universe.

—Hildegard of Bingen

Prayer ones the soul to God.

—Julian of Norwich

Seeds of Call and Community

Pondering

A friend of mine says that "we pray to God on Sunday and prey on our neighbor on Monday." His remark reveals a popular attitude toward prayer — that it is not part of daily life. In our dualistic culture it is typical to divide the personal from the political, the interior life from the exterior.

One way to bridge the divide of these two worlds is for us to pray together. In fact, for a growing number of people prayer in community is the central focus for their daily lives. Participants at the Franciscan School of Theology in Berkeley, for example, devote their Friday evenings to utter silence with attention and turning their lives over to the Creator. Some find that the Native American sweat lodge fosters prayer; in a lodge representing the womb of the Earth, in the presence of hot rocks and water poured over them, they pray for all members of the Earth community. Others are nourished by Eucharist and the Sunday liturgy as a communion of believers, of those on a shared way.

Today many feel a divine call but find no ecclesiastical or cultural context in which to realize their vocation. They need a "new religious order" for urban contemplatives, one that would furnish a communal context in which participants might find support for an examined life of prayer and reflection and that would promote relationship and friendship while honoring the wisdom, diversity and personal creativity of each member.

In such groups prayer becomes the very oxygen of life, the principle in which God becomes incarnate, the organizing principle that enables these groups to carry vitality and support into our broken world — to Bosnia, Jerusalem, Belfast, Quebec, Moscow, Johannesburg and to every field, fish, antelope and child.

Soulwork

Consider praying together with others on a regular basis. Find an environment and format that best suits your

Root relationships are developed between former strangers as each person listens for deepest fears and dreams, experiences the energy of "my heart was strangely warmed," and discovers focused energy in organized action.

—Richard Harmon,
Portland Organizing
Project

We can't wake up alone.
—Joanna Macy

group but be open to experimenting with a variety of formats. Here is one example of a group prayer experience: Gather at night. Provide a vigil candle for each participant. As each one's candle is lit, the leader invites that person to walk gently in silence while meditating on a verse like Meister Eckhart's, "If the only prayer you ever say is 'thank you,' that is enough."

After fifteen minutes all the participants return to the starting place (the leader may ring a bell) and form a circle, still holding their lighted candles. Those who wish are invited to share briefly some sense of their gratitude. Extinguish the candles together.

God is here
in this very place,
just as much incarnate
as in a human being
long ago.

—Meister Eckhart

Sooner or later something seems to call us
onto a particular path.

—James Hillman

30

Letter Writing

Pondering

I remember, as a child, listening to my Aunt Margaret read aloud her weekly letter from her brother Harry. The beginning was always the same: "I will now take a few minutes and write this letter."

Letter writing is an art. In an age of faxes, e-mail and telephones, the letter remains an important and irreplaceable avenue of communication. When I receive my mail each day, I first look for letters or postcards — any personal communications. There is something special about the written word that says, "I'm thinking of you; I care about you."

I have often been asked to write a letter on someone's behalf; I welcome these requests as opportunities to reveal how I feel about the persons and to highlight their gifts. In addition, it gives me time to focus on a particular person and recall how much his or her special talents and characteristics have brought appreciation into my life.

A letter, the written word, has the power to conjure up a friend who is absent. It is a gift of presence.

> Friendship requires not only commitment, but also communication. A good friendship feeds on a reaffirmation of the delicate bonds that unite . . . . I see letters I have received as sacraments, holy things, paper tabernacles that contain the love of my friends.
>
> —Edward Hays

Soulwork

Write a letter of recommendation for one of your friends. Doing so can strengthen your relationship and provide an opportunity for you to express your deepest feelings about the person. Share the letter with your friend, if you wish.

Write a letter of gratitude about a group or community of which you are a part. Describe how your relationship with this group enhances your life.

Write a letter expressing your appreciation to the area in which you live (your bioregion). Mention in particular the flora and fauna of your specific part of Earth.

What can you do for your friend Earth? Resolve to take some action, however small, on behalf of Earth this week.

> There is some part of your life that needs the other to complete itself.
>
> —John O'Donohue

31

Write a letter to yourself from Gaia (Earth). What does Gaia say to you?

We are already one but we imagine that we are not. What we have to recover is our original unity.

—Thomas Merton

Postcards and Packages:
Staying in Touch Through Letters and Food

Pondering

It was the end of August: School was starting, and memories of the past came bubbling forth. I remember how I, like young people today, went off to school — Assumption University of Windsor, Canada — to study Chemistry. What I remember even more than my classes and classmates are the messages I would receive from home.

My aunts would send me letters and on occasion a "care package" of my favorite cookies and strawberry tarts. As I look back, I realize that their letters and gifts were the way my family stayed with me even though we were no longer together.

As I reflect on the meaning of staying in touch with letters and food, I realize that as a Christian the same thing has happened to me. When Jesus left, we received letters (Scripture) and food (Eucharist). Today I have begun to understand that the "letters" are not only the scriptures of the Bible but are also the scripture of creation. In fact, a "sacramental spirituality" reminds us that everything, all of life, is revelatory. Everything is a reminder of and points toward the divine. As I and my friends were nourished by "care packages" we received from home when we were students, so also were we fed by our "soul food" that nourished our bodies and energized our spirits.

These thoughts came to me during the media coverage of the twentieth anniversary of the death of Elvis Presley. As I saw this event portrayed in the newspapers and on television, I realized that people were finding ways to be connected to Elvis twenty years after his death, through his music and memorabilia and by making trips to Graceland in Memphis. The phenomena seemed a powerful reminder of the deep feelings people have for yesterday, and a sign of our urgent quest for meaning and for something sacred in our lives. Perhaps, as one friend suggested, the powerful

> Let every word be the fruit of action and reflection . . . speak to make a new world possible.
>
> —Dom Helder Camara

> Real intimacy is a sacred experience.
>
> —John O'Donohue

> I can't myself raise the winds that might blow us, or that ship, into a better world. But I can at least put up the sail so that when the winds come, I can catch it.
>
> —E. F. Schumacher

interest in "Graceland Blues" is a commentary that our present cultural orientation, including traditional religion, is not meeting this need for meaning.

Soulwork

Take some time to write a postcard or letter to someone you care deeply about; perhaps sending that person a gift of his or her favorite food. Reflect on how these gifts make it possible for you to be present to your family or friends.

Take a walk in nature. Remember a special place — a lake, fields, mountains, ocean — that nourished your soul and spirit in your youth. Reflect on how positive aspects of creation remind you of the divine. Perhaps you might compose a poem or reflection from your connection making.

34

The Magic of a Child

Pondering

The phone rang at 9:30 P.M. It was my nephew, calling to announce the birth of his daughter, the firstborn to him and his wife.

The conversation was exhilarating; it seemed as if all the joy and expectation of the ages were present in the welcoming of this new life. This incarnation moment in the life of our family touched the extremities of my experience and my soul. As the new father told of his excitement, pain, pride and sense of the awesome responsibility that he and his wife had just assumed, comments from others tumbled into my consciousness.

I remembered the words of a friend: "Of all the things that have happened in my life — ordination, marriage, work — nothing has come close to the moment of the birth of my child."

The wisdom and grace in the words of Thomas Berry — "All of the work we do, we do for the children" — took on even greater meaning for me. This new arrival to the suburbs of Chicago has been a great teacher; her birth a life-changing event. Even the celebration of Christmas has been expanded and enhanced; it is no longer a history-bound event confined to a manger in a faraway land. Although it *is* that, of course, it is also a cosmic and continuous bringing forth of new life, something the universe does and we continue to wonder about. The incarnation is expressed in the bloom of a flower, the dawning of a new day, the emergence of a fresh idea — all such moments of birth share in the Birth at Bethlehem. Each "incarnation" reflects an experience of the cosmic Christ; we celebrate the pattern that connects and summons us into the fullness of being, the time in the future that will be marked by the coming of the new creation, the coming of the reign of God and the expression of a planetary Pentecost.

In the joy of the birth of this child I also remembered the words of a colleague: "I was at the birth of my sister's

> The child, instead of being a burden, shows himself to us as the greatest and most consoling of nature's wonders.
>
> —Maria Montessori

> What was extraordinary was that I saw clearly, indisputedly, finally, that the child, the grass, the trees, the sky about were all woven of the same material, were all part of the same fabric, which was the fabric of which the universe is made.
>
> —Sharon Butala

A new kind of life is
starting.

—Teilhard de Chardin

first child, and I was with my father when he died. I can't tell you how similar these two events were." Yes, the moments of beginning and ending are in some way simultaneous and deeply connected. I remember at liturgy one day, Rosie talked about being with her sister when she gave birth to her daughter — and about being with her father when he died. She said that she was amazed at how similar were the two experiences. As she spoke, it struck me that in the evolutionary process of the universe sex and death came into existence at the same time. The proximity of death and birth reveal the depth and meaning that each brings. Both birth and sex require a kind of death experience, a letting go in order that life may happen. Death can also be understood as a birth, a birth into the next phase of our journey. At the interface of life and death, the depth of the great paradoxical truth of the paschal mystery is revealed.

Death borders upon our
birth, and our cradle
stands in the grave.

—Bishop Hall, 1574-1656

I am grateful today for the phone call I received from my nephew, for the good news of new life, for the refreshed perspective on the meaning of incarnation, for the connection that unites sex, birth and death in the unfolding of the cosmos and of each of us.

The following words are part of a Native American (Omaha) ritual welcoming a child to the cosmos:

Ho! ye Sun, Moon, Stars, all ye that move in the heavens,
I bid you hear me! Into your midst has come a new life.
    Consent ye, I implore, make its path smooth,
    that it may reach the brow of the first hill.
Ho! ye Winds, Clouds, Rain, all ye that move in the air,
I bid you hear me! Into your midst has come a new life.
    Consent ye, I implore, make its path smooth,
    that it may reach the brow of the second hill.
Ho! ye Hills, Rivers, all ye of the earth,
I bid you hear me! Into your midst has come a new life.
    Consent ye, I implore, make its path smooth,
    that it may reach the brow of the third hill.
Ho! ye Birds, great and small, that fly in the air,
Ho! ye Animals, great and small, that dwell in the forest,
Ho! ye Insects, that creep among the grasses,
I bid you hear me! Into your midst has come a new life.
    Consent ye, I implore, make its path smooth,

that it may reach the brow of the fourth hill.
Ho! all ye of the heavens, all ye of the air, all ye of the earth,
I bid you hear me! Into your midst has come a new life.
Consent ye, I implore, make its path smooth,
. . . then shall it travel beyond the four hills.

Soulwork

Spend some time meditating on birth. Look at your baby pictures. Ask your parents about the events of your infancy. Invite them to share any stories that they have been told about their own early days. Share with your children your experience of their birth.

Then reflect on an experience of death — a parent, relative, friend, public figure.

Finally, meditate on the connection between birth and death. How are they similar? How is the reality that sex and death come into existence along with birth significant for your life journey? How can you "give birth" to yourself? What spiritual practices do you feel called to undertake to help you in this process of personal "birthing"?

It Takes a Universe

The child awakens to a universe. The mind of a child to a world of meaning. Imagination to a world of beauty. Emotions to a world of intimacy.

It takes a universe
to make a child both
in outer form and inner
spirit. It takes
a universe to educate
a child. A universe
to fulfill a child.

Each generation presides over the meeting of these two in the succeeding generation. Thus our nursery rhymes. These early rhymes, these early stories, are the most profound,
most lovely,
most delightful sources of guidance and inspiration the child will ever have.

"Star light, star bright..."
how memorable, inspiring,
instructive, these verses
of Robert Lewis Stevenson
from the later years
of the last century.

So now we write our own verses, bringing the child and the universe into their mutual fulfillment.

While the stars ring out in
the heavens.

—Thomas Berry

Birthdays

Pondering

Birthday images flood into my memories. I'm four, in front of a cake in my mother's home. I'm thirty-four, surrounded by friends in Mario's Restaurant in Toronto's Annex. My birthday is September 6. When I was in grade school I was sad on the eve of my birthday because it usually coincided with Labor Day and going back to school.

On my desk is a picture of me with two of my aunts and my father. They are holding out gifts and cards. It's my twenty-fourth birthday. As I examine the photo, I think of these members of my family and wonder what they thought about birthdays.

Birthdays are times of joy and longing, gratitude and regret. They remind us of the universal desire to experience rebirth; we celebrate both new life and life's renewal. On our birthdays we look back on our origins and feel grateful to our parents for the gifts of life.

But even as we celebrate life's beginning, we are inevitably reminded of life's ending — of *our* ending. Yes, paradoxically, birthdays are also moments to contemplate death. From the traumatic moment that ushered us forth from the womb, the reality of the tomb becomes ever closer and more present in our lives. The deep rhythms of the paschal mystery, of life, death and rebirth, permeate our existence. Death begins at the moment of birth.

Soulwork

While birthdays are special days, any day is an appropriate time to express your gratitude for the gift of life you have received. Pick a day this week to celebrate life. Invite family and friends to gather "just for fun." Find a way to thank each one for the joy and support he or she has brought to your life.

Oh, turn and be born again, and walk the road and find once more the lost path.

—Antonio Machado

Blessing Prayer for a Birthday

God of Life,
bless *(name)* and
each of us
with wisdom,
the wisdom you shared
with your clever son,
Pablo Picasso, artist
and lover of life,
who said, "It takes a
long, long time for
one to become
young."
Make us younger on
each birthday.
Open our eyes to
wonder and awe;
delight our hearts with
amazement and
playfulness.

—Edward Hays

The Family

Pondering

As we look at the family from the vantage point of the new millennium, I realize that there is much to learn and ponder. The family is the basic unit of society. It is in the family that our lives are shaped, that we achieve a sense of self. It is within our family that we discover our identity, learn our place and hear our call.

The family is the source of depth and spirituality; grace erupts from the interaction of parents, children and extended members. Family life at the precipice of the new millennium is in a delicate and dangerous place. Our culture is filled with fractured relationships, and nowhere is this more clearly seen and felt than in the family. Divorce is commonplace. Focused by the O. J. Simpson trial, we are all too aware of the painful reality that domestic violence is the number-one crime in North America. Pedophilia, the pathological assault on the young and defenseless ones, is becoming more widely known and more widespread. The complexity of contemporary family life, with both parents usually working and everyone in the family generally over-extended, makes it difficult to realize dreams and have needs met. The very language "nuclear family" reveals a worldview that sees reality as machinelike. In fact, the term "nuclear family" suggests a perspective of the father, mother and child as the atoms, the basic building blocks of our society: a closed system that tends to separate home from work, love from life, parent from child and husband from wife.

Modern science sheds light on this problem. If the nuclear family is a closed system, like the Dead Sea, in which nothing flows in and nothing flows out, we need a new family structure that is open to new energies and change, like the Sea of Galilee, where new lifestyles, new relationships and new possibilities can be born here at the precipice of the twenty-first century. We are challenged to create structures that encourage mutual respect and under-

> We believe the family to be the greatest source of the will, the energy and the resourcefulness necessary to generate lasting societal change as we approach the twenty-first century.
>
> — *Journal of Family Life*

> If you really converse with people [and, we might add, the Earth], you learn so much. So much wisdom, so much suffering.
>
> —Leonardo Boff

> We have all known the long loneliness and we have learned that the only solution is love that comes with community.
>
> —Dorothy Day

standing, that make the family a place where life is given, love experienced and tradition passed on.

Perhaps we can best begin by returning to an essential understanding of the nature of the family as expressed in the trinitarian context of Western Christianity. This deep truth, also revealed by the universe story, is that there are three principles and tendencies that are inherent in family life and that, in fact, permeate all of existence: differentiation, interiority and communion.

Differentiation invites us to honor the uniqueness present in each member of the family; to celebrate the particular moment of each person's creativity and accomplishments. For example: birthdays, anniversaries, moments of maturation and more.

The principle of *interiority* invites us to rejoice in the particular personality of each family member; to express reverence and respect for the mystery present in each person and revealed in the wonder and fascination of that unique interior life.

The principle of *communion* challenges us to develop deep connections with each of the members of our families. Communion is the language of relationship, and the family is the primary context where functional relationships are fostered and alienation is healed.

Whenever these principles are present, our families flourish and the divine is in our midst. Moreover, when we practice these principles in the family, we gain the capacity to extend our sense of family. We discover our place on the planet as sacred and strive to live our lives in rhythm with the cycles of the seasons. We deepen our awareness of the spiritual dimension that is present throughout the universe as we embrace the mystery and beauty of the natural world. A good model of family life lived within the story of the universe is found in these words of the African bushmen: "Remember, little cousin, everything in the bush has its own right to be there — we are all bound to recognize and respect it as we wish our own right to be recognized and respected...." One is never alone in the bush.

Happiness is an inside job.

—John Powell

The greatest lessons I have learned as a familied person have been those of community. Not only have I learned to exist reasonably (or not so reasonably) under the same roof with a variety of personalities, not only have I learned that it takes time and effort and communication skills to negotiate in community, I have also learned that at the root of community, there is the mystery of communion, the mystery that together we are the body of Christ.

—Wendy Wright

40

Soulwork

Take some time each day to practice the trinitarian principles in your family. How do you celebrate the differences among the members of your family? What is your response to each of the unique personalities in your family? In what ways are you developing and deepening relationships among family members?

Reflect on your ancestral roots. What customs and traditions have you inherited from your family of origin? How were they passed on to you? Are you passing them on?

Reflect on the sources of what bind you together as a family (communion) — as well as the unique gifts that differentiate each person in your family.

Tell your family story to your children and grandchildren or to other youngsters, perhaps in a school or club context. Introduce them to the flora and fauna of your region.

Take time today to honor the sacredness and the beauty of the natural world — and the "beauty" inherent in your family.

In friendship the first act is always an act of recognition.

—John O'Donohue

If the great unknowable mystery of God is pictured as the glowing sun, and God incarnate as a ray of that same streaming to the Earth, then spirit is the point of light that actually arrives and affects the Earth with warmth and energy.

—Elizabeth Johnson

The Wisdom of the Body

Pondering

We live in a society prone to look to experts to define our true meaning. Yet it is struggling with our own experience that is one of our strongest sources of wisdom and contact with the divine. Reflection, prayer, meditation and being with the processes of life — all enrich the soul, validate our journey and celebrate our destiny.

A significant part of our personal experience lies in the experience of our bodies. There is a wisdom of the body that can be a guide to choices, decision-making, and even to life directions. When we have questions about our work, our friendships, our future, sitting quietly, focusing on an issue and listening to our bodily response can lead us to insights or indicate a spiritual direction. Today is a day to honor the body and the wisdom that lies within.

Return to the land means recovering something of the biorhythms of the body, the day, and the seasons from the world of clocks, computers and artificial lighting that have always alienated us from these biorhythms.

—Rosemary Radford Ruether

Soulwork

Meditate today on the being that you are. Begin by allowing your awareness to focus on your body. Relax. Become aware of your breathing. Concentrate on relaxing each part of your body from the tips of your toes to the top of your head. Let the tension flow out of your muscles. Feel yourself becoming calmer and calmer.

As you sink into this deep relaxation, ask how you can reverence your body in a new way. Perhaps you might promise yourself that you will no longer pollute, punish or neglect the health and wholeness of your body or the body of Earth. Other suggestions for using your body as a vehicle for peace and an instrument of celebration include:

Good is the body from
    cradle to grave,
Sensing the sunlight,
    the rug to the ground.
Feeling, perceiving,
    within and around,
Good is the body from
    cradle to grave,
Good is the flesh that
    the word has become.

—Christopher Wren

- Exercising regularly
- Getting adequate rest
- Taking nature walks
- Being present to the sun
- Drinking pure water
- Eating healthy and wholesome food

♦ Reflecting regularly on the Earth as the body of God, a source of sacredness and strength.

The human venture is a
   daydream
Of what is most real and
   promising in life
A nightmare of what
   frightens me most
A rude awakening
A challenge to self-
   acceptance
A challenge to struggle
A challenge to walk
   though the netherworld
Of our own unconscious
To articulate, tremble,
   and rejoice
To reach for life
And become grounded
   and grateful
For life on the gorgeous
   planet.[1]

Love

Pondering

Love is a great mystery. St. Paul writes: "There are three things that last — faith, hope and love. The greatest of these is love."

Love is an attraction. The expression *falling in love* indicates a magnetic attraction toward someone, a force that drives us forward into life, consistently and sometimes unbidden.

But love is also more than attraction; it is intention, a consistent act of the will that reflects nobility and sacrifice. Love can bring out the best in us. Love is not exclusive. It can warm our family, grow out of friendship, even be extended to other species.

Love is mystical; it involves a oneness with the beloved. Love takes us beyond ourselves and makes us more, makes life more. Whenever I meet someone who is "in love," I feel inspired. My life seems to expand. I see things differently and seem to love myself in a deeper and more expansive way.

The whole universe teaches us about love through the mysterious attraction of gravitation. Each river, rock and tree is drawn forward in its own particular way. The universe also demonstrates that there is a particularity to love. Each member of the Earth community falls in love in its own particular way. In a sense, love *is* blind; it is deeper than conscious choice, mysterious and surprising.

Love carries us forward into life.
It awakens the spirit and cultivates the soul.

Love inspires and challenges.
It opens the heart and cultivates the soul.

Love is that quality of living
That multiplies possibilities and cultivates the soul.

Love is a preoccupation with self-transcendence
A deep-seated attraction in the soul.

Love is as strong as death.

—Song of Songs 8: 6

Love alone can unite living beings so as to complete and fulfill them, for it alone joins them by what is deepest in themselves . . . .Love is the free and imaginative outpouring of the Spirit over all unexplored paths.

—Teilhard de Chardin

This is what you shall do: Love the Earth and Sun and the animals . . . and your very flesh shall be a great poem.

—Walt Whitman

44

Love calls us to community
And celebrates our destiny and call.

Soulwork

Reflect on one or two relationships in your life in which love is an especially binding force. Reflect on other areas of your life in which the term *love* might apply: your work, a hobby, a life dream, a favorite natural setting or area of the country.

I was exploring Mount Tamalpais in northern California one evening. As I rested on a stone ledge, I noticed a small plaque over my shoulder. It read:

Give me these hills where I find love.
I ask no more of heaven.

Have you experienced such an unexpected gift from Earth? Take some time today to draw strength from these personal Earth gifts. Or reflect upon your place of origin and celebrate its beauty and richness, the contribution it has made to your life.

The door to the world is the heart.

—Corita Kent

It is spring again. The Earth is like a child that knows poems by heart.

—Rainer Maria Rilke

We need to develop the ability to love until it embraces the totality of the people of the Earth.... We have reached a decisive point in human evolution at which the only way forward is in the direction of a common passion, a "conspiration." Love, then, is a sacred reserve of energy; it is like the blood of spiritual evolution.

—Teilhard de Chardin

45

II.

Shattering

You who by constantly shattering our mental categories,
force us to go ever further and further
in pursuit of truth.

—Teilhard de Chardin

Accept surprises that upset your plans
Shatter your dreams
Give a completely different turn to your day
And . . . who knows . . . to your life.
It is not chance.
Leave the Father free to weave the pattern of your days.

—Dom Helder Camara

Losing a species to extinction
Is like tearing a page
Out of Sacred Scripture.

—Calvin DeWitt

46

Darkness

Pondering

The mystery of the seasons and the rhythm of night and day enchant me. The darkness is a particular mystery; for me, it involves the frightening, the hidden and the unexpected.

John of the Cross wrote about what he called "the dark night of the soul." This expression seems particularly apt when my accomplishments seem only an illusion; when I lie awake at night dreading the morning and wondering if it will ever come; when existence seems meaningless.

Spiritual guides over the years claim that the primary response to these dark nights is not to fight them but to go deeply into the experience while at the same time taking good care of ourselves. Morning *will* come. The dark night does not last forever, and eventually light will come out of the darkness. We will emerge feeling cleansed of false perceptions. Our false ego will be "reformed," and our true self stronger.

Cultures can experience a "dark night" too. As collapse and devastation proliferate around us, we must surrender our pathological way of life and seek out a new vision. The legacy of John of the Cross is a particular gift as we struggle with these defining moments at the end of the second millennium. Perhaps it is true that the darkest hour *is* before dawn; if so, we have much to look forward to, much to anticipate, much to let go of, and much for which to hope. Ours is a time of renaissance and rebirth.

Soulwork

Give yourself a day of solitude, a time of "sitting still at the precipice." Make it a day to be with nature, yourself and God. Ponder your life's journey, your questions, pains, understandings and misunderstandings, your gifts, unresolved emotions, hopes, fascinations, accomplishments. In the face of the "dark night," create an inner space for seeds of rebirth to germinate.

All of us have mileposts that indicate the evolution of

> The ground of the soul is dark.
>
> —Meister Eckhart

> Mysticism is the necessary spiritual antecedent for global peace.
>
> —Jim Forrest on the thought of Thomas Merton

> The most beautiful thing a person can say about God would be for that person to remain silent from the wisdom of an unseen wealth.
>
> —Meister Eckhart

our spiritual journey; they mark our relationship to our destiny and to our God. It is important to mark such transitional moments in our lives with ritual — to create images, music, movement, humor, community. Take time now to plan (or recall) an important event in your life and celebrate it.

It's a pity there are people who will go through life never having thought of watching a sunrise.

—Dom Helder Camara

Evil and Pain

Pondering

The question of evil is a great puzzle to me. An insight from Professor Patrick Flood, my freshman philosophy teacher, however, has remained with me to this day. It went something like this: *Philosophers, theologians, and others have struggled with the question of evil for many years; their response continues to be that it remains a mystery.* So it isn't surprising that evil remains a puzzle to me.

> He who has not visited the house of pain has seen but half the universe.
> —Ralph Waldo Emerson

Classical theologians have named our struggle with evil, pain, darkness and silence the *via negativa*. They have offered us a spiritual strategy for dealing with the bitter and burdensome aspects of life. From this perspective we come to see that pain, for example, is an integral aspect of life; it is more than a phenomenon to be diagnosed and medicated. Rather, it is a mystery to be lived. Pain can be understood as a result of evil. But it can also be the result of our finiteness, the limits of our human condition. To some extent pain comes to us as a result of our unwillingness to embrace the limits of our lives.

Our response to pain depends on our spirituality. A healthy spirituality involves avoiding two extremes. One is denial, which may lead to substance abuse or some other destructive behavior. The other extreme is an inordinate attachment to pain. Here we cling to pain as a substitute for pleasure. This can lead to a great deal of confusion.

> We get *through* the pain of our lives, not over it or around it.
> —Joe Nassal, CPPS

An authentic spirituality will help us distinguish pleasure from pain; we learn to experience pain for its own sake but then let it go. Meister Eckhart teaches us this practice:

> When one has learned
> to let go
> and let be
> then one is well disposed
> and he or she is always in the right place
> within the society or in solitude.

A spirituality that embraces life's *via negativa* involves acknowledging and living within the limits of the

> There is no birth of consciousness without pain.
> —Carl Jung

49

human condition and, in particular, within the limits of our own gifts. This does not mean denigrating ourselves or denying our possibilities but being at peace with who we are. Such a spirituality means letting go of illusion, acknowledging mystery and being willing to learn and change. It teaches us that pain can strengthen us and deepen our capacity to embrace life.

Over the years I have often thought about my philosophy teacher's response to the question of evil. I thought about it again when I read Abrahm's *A Shadow in America*, another attempt to enter this mystery. My own disappointments and darkness are yet another window on the question.

Indeed, many of us are in the middle of a stormy search for our true self. Tragedy, doubt and annihilation abound around the globe. Within this framework we are pilgrims, people whose lives are crowded with spiritual emergencies that, when properly understood, are opportunities for expanding and deepening our journey. Moments of upheaval can be reminders of God's action in our lives, invitations to a more profound awareness and experience of the divine.

We can even feel abandoned by God. As we reflect on the pain of lost friendship, lost direction and lost love, we search for the promise in such hurt. Our reflection teaches us that such moments are potentially moments of transformation when we can come home to ourselves and to our God. Being lost is, after all, a precondition for being found.

Soulwork

Attend to a physical, emotional or spiritual pain in your life with an attitude of "lightness," with reverence toward its mystery. Hold a prayerful attitude of openness to God's movement in that mystery.

Today, confront the shadows in your life. Do a "spring cleaning" of your psyche by looking at your buried secrets and opening them to the fresh air of conscious exploration and openness. Pray for the courage to reverse old patterns that encourage you to dramatize past hurts; pray for the courage to find new ways of being.

I will make the whole earth my altar and on it will offer you all the labors and sufferings of the world.

—Teilhard de Chardin

Pick some daisies.
Share them.
Keep a promise.
Explore the unknown.
Reach out.
Let someone in.
Hug a kid.
Slow down.
See a sunrise.
Listen to the rain.
Trust life.
Have faith.
Enjoy.
Make a mistake.
Learn from it.
Laugh.

From Pathology to Promise

Pondering

I have many memories of my participation in a psycho-therapeutic community in Toronto named Therafields. When someone was ill, having family problems, or otherwise in crisis, our community would gather and create a circle of energy on the person's behalf. As we held hands, conscious of the energy moving from hand to body to hand, we would visualize our collective energy forming a cone of white light to cleanse, purify and protect the one for whom we were praying.

I can't explain what happened during those sessions, but I know it was something important. In a world often overwhelmed with destructive energy, permeated with violence and abuse, we need such strategies to keep our souls alive.

As we strive to confront the depths of the cultural pathology that surrounds us, our spirituality must include some way of cleansing, purifying and protecting so that we may confront the negative energies and embrace the possibilities of life.

I always remember Good Friday as such a time. We said the Rosary, went to church, watched at noon and remembered the dead. Good Friday is a celebration not of dismal depression but of joy and pain and liberation. Good Friday is about transforming our lives; it is about transition and new beginnings. It is also about alienation. Jesus' passion transformed pain, death and denial into life, hope and the promise of the Resurrection. The challenge of Good Friday is to transform the pathology of our culture into the promise of passion for new life.

The word *pathology* literally means "the study of suffering," yet the dominant meaning in our society is that something is wrong. Dorothy Sölle reminds us that the root meaning of *apathy* is "*not* being able to suffer."

The sky and the earth failed
at the time of Christ's dying
because he too was part of nature.
Thus those who were his friends
suffered pain
because they loved him.

—Julian of Norwich

Soulwork

Form a group and make the "secular stations of the cross" (visiting places where oppression occurs in our time). Before setting your route, meet to discuss where crucifixion happens today in your area. Where are the temples of oppression? What powers call out for your worship? What forces impinge upon you? What forces of alienation invite your participation? Some places for your consideration are banks that invest in oppressive regimes; sites where nuclear warheads are made; laboratories where inhumane experiments are conducted; welfare offices that demean and embarrass the poor they serve; any actions that endanger the unborn of any species. What does Christ's model of dealing with such forces offer you as a pattern for confronting these issues of pathology?

Take time today to reflect upon what is transpiring in your life. Look at what is engaging you on a very deep and confrontative level. What is calling you to life? Take this opportunity to drink deeply of life and to feel the pain and possibility of life's unfolding.

The damaged Earth, violent and unjust social structures, the lonely and broken heart — all cry out for a fresh start. In the midst of this suffering, the Creator Spirit, through the mediation of created powers, comes, as the Pentecost sequence sings, to wash what is unclean; to pour water on what is drought-stricken; to heal what is hurt; to loosen what is rigid; to warm what is freezing; to straighten out what is crooked and bent.

—Elizabeth Johnson

Death

Pondering

As I stood at the bedside of my mother, her body ravaged by cancer, the reality of mortality came thundering home to me: the separation, termination, loss, mystery and inevitableness of it all. I was eighteen.

With my mother's death, followed later by that of my father, the line to eternity was now open to me and my siblings. We were next. As the decades have moved along, the reality of death has brushed up against me more and more frequently.

It is not easy to embrace death as an integral part of life, especially in a culture that does everything possible to deny its very existence. Our society promotes face lifts, tummy tucks, vitamins to extend life. We spend billions of dollars to deny death and its harbinger — age. Wrinkles and gray hair are not to be tolerated; we aspire in all things to be "youthful." We even discuss death in euphemisms: he "made his transition"; she "went to the other side"; they "passed on."

The post-Vatican funeral liturgy, which uses white vestments and pronouncements about the Resurrection, stands in stark opposition to a society that looks upon death with despair and denial.

Yet the natural world can teach us much about the meaning and art of dying. The death of stars gave us the Earth; the death of procaryotes gave us oxygen; the many "deaths" of winter bring us the life of spring, and so on.

Death is integral to the life process. It is thus not to be denied; rather it asks to be accepted and embraced in its mystery. It is preceded by life (incarnation) and followed by new life (resurrection). It is present in every tradition and fully embodied in the rhythms of the natural world. In its fullest form, it is a mystery, a reality, a prayer. Hopefully it is a daily occurrence, as we die to ourselves and rise to concern for others. Properly understood, death is life's most radical act, its fullest expression. It should be embraced, not

> ...now, at the end of my life, I can stand on the peak I have scaled and continue to look ever more closely into the future, and there with ever more assurance, see the ascent of God.
>
> —Teilhard de Chardin

> Death is a process of cosmic resorption. . . in the sense that the cosmic elements dissolve into one another.
>
> —Mircea Eliade

feared, so that life can be lived more fully.

Death is about letting go into mystery, into the universe. It is about coming to terms with the limits of life. It is both challenge and possibility.

Soulwork

What feelings do you have about your own death? How do you understand the phrase, "We die into life"?

To die to anger, resentment and cynicism allows us to sink deeply into our appreciation of life and find there a profound possibility for peace and a profound appreciation of the source of our pain. What feelings do you need to acknowledge and let go of today? What have you avoided facing? Reflect upon those things that you are clutching to yourself that prevent you from moving to a fuller, more loving way of life.

Remember this:
That when God
releases the soul
it sinks down
and gives thanks
even for this.

—Mechtild of
Magdeburg

The tragedy of life is
not death, but what we
let die inside us while
we live.

—Norman Cousins

I believe in the sun
even when the sun is not
shining.
I believe in God
even when God is silent.

—written on a wall of a
Nazi concentration camp

54

Funerals

Pondering

Sister Nancy asked me to celebrate the funeral liturgy for Sister Madeline. It was a privilege.

There was something in the air that evening; a joyful mood of resurrection permeated the room/chapel. Ann read from the *Divine Milieu* (in French); Sister Joanne reflected on Sister Madeline's life and read excerpts from her journal. The cheerfulness was palpable.

This woman from France, who had been involved in Catholic Action, educated as a biologist, friend of Teilhard de Chardin, teacher, mentor, sister and friend, had now died. Along with the pain of separation she had left us all a gift: a life that was a positive, hope-filled moment and experience of resurrection. It was a great gift on which to contemplate. It gave us strength to carry on with the work of our own lives and to face our own deaths.

That evening I thought about the funerals that had marked my life — my mother's funeral when I was eighteen; my father's funeral, where I was the celebrant; my Aunt Margaret's funeral, where I was the homilist. I remember my brother commenting on how I must have spent a lot of time preparing the homily for Aunt Margaret. I said that no I hadn't; all I had done was share with others the vision I had learned and the pain I had felt at the loss of someone we had all loved. Funerals are benchmarks. We all die — celebrity, family member, friend, homeless person on the streets. From some, like Sister Madeline, we receive special gifts — in her case, cheerfulness and courage — that teach us how to live and how to die. Their funerals witness to the joy of resurrection.

> I am not dying, I am entering life.
>
> —St. Thérèse of Lisieux on her deathbed

> You will never understand death until it comes to your door.
>
> —Irish Saying

Soulwork

A powerful spiritual exercise is to compose your own eulogy. Spend some time writing a statement of who you are, how you want to be remembered. Keep your eulogy and reread it occasionally during a time of reflection. It can help you to clarify who you want to be in your present life situation, and can keep you on track.

This exercise is very effective as a group activity. If you are part of a group, allow time for each participant to write his or her eulogy. Then each person can select a group member to read aloud the eulogy. The person being eulogized might lie on a table or platform, with eyes closed, while the eulogy is read. Some of the group members stand around the "bier" with their right hands on the person. When the eulogy is finished, the other group members ring bells and beat drums as the reader assists the "dead" person to rise and be welcomed by each group member. Work through the group members in turn until all have "died" and "risen."

Although not in the form of a eulogy, the following reflection resulted from my own thoughts about my death:

I Want to Be Remembered
(Looking Back Toward the Twenty-First Century)

I want to be remembered as someone who:

lived in such a way that when death came, it could be embraced without regret . . .

lived, loved and risked, yet continued to discover hope in the struggle, so that in looking back there will be no "what ifs" — or at least only a few . . .

honored and revered the sacred impulse to pass something on so that the world can be a better place for the children . . .

faced fear, saw in pain the possibility to grow, let go of grudges, strove to forgive and always was open to life's deeper meaning while avoiding the temptation to cynicism or despair . . .

savored my time on Earth as a sacred presence and a moment of grace, who recognized the need for struggle and constant engagement while at the same time realizing that the outcome of our life is often a gift of the divine rather than a result of our effort . . .

touched others' lives and contributed to their journey while not in any way diminishing their existence for my own satisfaction or personal gain . . .

cared deeply and let others know it, felt pain and

56

learned from it, dared to be creative and was
surprised by it, and strove for justice and
made it possible for others . . .

longed for the sacredness of home, extended hospitality
to others and overcame obstacles so that finally I
could rest . . .

celebrated and honored the beauty of Earth,
experienced the enchantment of every place that I
saw and touched — especially the bioregion of my
birth, the St. Clair River and the trees, flowers,
fields, and seasons of southwestern Ontario, Canada . . .

was true to my calling, embraced the ambiguity of
existence, and strove to awaken to the paradoxes of
life — those puzzling paradoxes of marriage, priesthood,
community engagement and academia, solitude
and interaction, surrender and persistent effort —
resulting in a narrative of self-discovery where deep
peace abounds and life can become whole again . . .

dared to identify with the "inappropriate," resisted
conformity, chose to be on the edge and responded
fully to the summons of contradiction and synthesis
from where I discovered the courage and capacity
to be who I was supposed to be . . .

welcomed death not as a stranger but as a trusted
context of cosmic return to my origins, that place
whence the journey deepens and continues . . .

put hope before heartache, trust before terror and
possibility before problems . . .

is not forgotten at death,
though my genes live not in others,

whose capacity to code the culture was found
in green grass, a stately tree, clean water, the beauty
of a flower, and the smile and exuberance of
a child . . .

fostered hope, was committed to tomorrow and
generated "oxygen for the soul" while fostering
friendship in and through Earth.

Blessed are those for whom autumn's golden hymn of death is reveille. Blessed are those who are awakened to how short is the time left in their lives for generosity, heroism and affection . . . a reminder to value more keenly the gifts of their lives.

—Edward Hays

The Soul of Two Icons

Pondering

The television station interrupted its regular programming. Breaking news announced that a tragic auto accident had taken place in Paris and that one of the passengers in the ill-fated vehicle was Princess Diana of England. Two hours later the grim news followed: Diana was dead.

The announcement came startlingly into the consciousness of the peoples of the United Kingdom, North America and, in fact, all the world. As I sat saddened in my apartment on August 30, 1997, I wondered about the significance of this tragic event.

Somehow, in my mind's eye, I went back to an afternoon in November of 1963. I was playing handball during recreation at St. Peter's Seminary in London, Ontario. I remembered, like it was yesterday, a fellow student, Joe, telling us that President John F. Kennedy had fallen victim to an assassin's bullet during a motorcade procession through the streets of Dallas, Texas. It seemed that for the next number of endless days we were glued to the television as we watched in shock the wake, funeral and international responses that followed this dreadful deed. Now, some thirty-four years later, a parallel event had again broken onto the world stage.

As I looked back, I realized that in many ways both these people who spent too brief a time with us were reminders of the longings, fears and accomplishments that reside in all our minds and hearts.

So I asked myself: What was it about Diana that so captured the imaginations of a generation? What was it about this young woman borne into affluence and thrust upon the world stage at the age of twenty that made her such a target for the news through the years and particularly at this hour?

While imperfect, as each of us, Diana was and remains a mythological figure, an icon. Her beauty and affluence contributed to her image. She seemed to have everything,

It seems to me you
    lived your life
Like a candle in the wind
Never fading with the
    sunset
Or when the rains
    came ....
Your candle burned out
    long before
Your legend ever will.

—Elton John

Death is not a necessary last termination; it is a transformation into a more wholistic way of being.

—Diarmuid O'Murchu

58

destined to be the "Queen" of England. Yet she lacked what every person so desperately wants: love. She was a rebel in a tired institution. She seemed to make the "royals" real and available to the "common" person, and she experienced the pain and backlash of resistance to her efforts. She seemed strong, confident and committed. She touched the "leper," and she touched the hearts of millions. Yet she lived like a prisoner in her castle, estranged from her former husband and the institution of the monarchy. The media pursued her everywhere. There was a fascination with her every move. A young woman of beauty and promise, she left us all too soon.

As I reflected on the death of Diana, I remember standing on the main street of my hometown, Sombra, in Ontario. All the children of our two-room school, School Section #7, stood watching as Queen Elizabeth and the duke of Edinborough drove by. Even then it seemed healthy to have the head of state (the queen) distant from the head of government (the prime minister). I have always felt pleased that Canada and Great Britain made this distinction, while the president of the United States had to deal with both the duties of office and the overexposed celebrity of being head of state.

Yet Diana, who was not the queen, and would never have been, was in fact, as she so deeply desired, "the Queen of People's Hearts." Rejected in love, she dared to love; rich and famous, she still reached out to the poor and forgotten; embraced by the structure of the monarchy, she chose to be a reformer and to challenge the presupposition of her own inheritance; cast aside from a marriage and the child of a broken home, she maintained a sense of dignity and grace.

The tragic crash that ended her life at the young age of thirty-six can be a wake-up call for each of us as we strive to live fully and with gratitude the precious moments of our existence.

On the eve of Diana's funeral, we learned of the passing of Mother Teresa of Calcutta at age eighty-seven. She had founded a religious community dedicated to the dignity of the poor dying in India and throughout the world.

That whoever is sore
wounded by love
will never be made whole
unless
she embraces the very
same love
which wounded her.

—Mechtild of
Magdeburg

The question was not Diana or Mother Teresa. The question is what was happening in people To make them respond the way they did.

—Jim Wallis

Also a transformer, Mother Teresa had changed her life dramatically as she followed the impulse to serve the frail and most forgotten of God's people. She truly became a living icon, a model of dedication, determination and loving service.

I recall the time Mother Teresa and Diana actually met and the powerful image of them standing together. These two women, in many ways contrasting figures in regard to age, stature, appearance and lifestyle, found each other in life and captured the imagination of all of us in death.

Soulwork

What do you think Diana meant when she said, "I want to be the queen of people's hearts"?

How do you respond to Mother Teresa's acceptance speech for the Nobel Peace Prize: "On behalf of the poor, forgotten and dying, I accept"?

Who are the people in your life who evoke in you a response similar to what you feel about Diana and Teresa?

Meditate on the life of Mother Teresa, whose work and very existence were so unconditionally dedicated to the poor. What have you learned from the poor people you have known?

Gustavo Gutierrez, liberation theologian, declared that God is closer to the poor, not because they're better, but simply because they're poor! What do you think about this comment?

Ours is to be a free service to the poor.

—Mother Teresa

Anyone who has become aware of the injustices caused by the unfair division of wealth, must, if she has a heart, listen to the silent or violent protests of the poor.

—Dom Herder Camara

Injustice

Pondering

There is so much pain, so much of the cross, in the profound experience of humans' inhumanity to each other. Confronting cruelty and injustice, we face one of the most profound crises of soul that life can present. Injustice makes us feel that all is lost, that life is unfair, that there is nothing to hold onto.

Yet in the midst of our anger, pain and confusion, we also need to remember that the Spirit of Resurrection is present even — and sometimes, it seems, especially — in the most intolerable of conditions. The reign of God comes alive in countless heroic acts in Nazi concentration camps and Central American villages; in Ireland and Bosnia; in the midst of famine and political upheaval.

We are called to fight injustice with all our being; the Gospel is clear. But we often must relinquish the outcome to God and be grateful for the wisdom and guidance that we receive. As always, the cross and salvation intersect.

Soulwork

Make the cross and the resurrection come alive by listening to the story of a victim of injustice, a victim who has come through it with an enlarged soul. Read one of the following: *The Diary of Anne Frank*, the brief biography of Franz Jägerstätter, Maximillian Kolbe,[2] Etty Hillesum, or another account that interests you.

Justice demands
that we seek and find
the stranger, the broken,
the prisoner,
and comfort them.

—Mechtild of
Magdeburg

Whatever God does,
the first outburst
is always compassion.

—Meister Eckhart

Reformation

Pondering

Television programming is indicative of the pathology that permeates our culture. There is a sameness that denies the value of the unique and clings to the familiar, however trite and overdone. The artist stands isolated, sidelined from the mainstream of society and life. In the absence of creativity and in the avoidance of spontaneity, mystery is denigrated and truth-telling becomes a rare practice.

As we stand on our cultural precipice, flooded with possibilities and hope, a necessary first step to an authentic reformation is gratitude for the diverse gifts of our gorgeous planet. This disposition sets us on our way toward internal transformation. We need to let go of familiar but out-moded institutions and to create new and diverse vehicles that honor the richness of creation, the richness of God's word to us.

Together we can make a place on the planet where young and old, rich and poor, teachers and pupils can join hands and march into the future with confidence in the power of their individual abilities. Through conscientious use of the mass media, banks, monetary funds, housing, agriculture, transportation and lifestyle choices we can take back the soul of the culture. Only through such integrated efforts will our society and the worldview that guides it be *re-formed* so that we can move into a future that will dissolve meaninglessness, emptiness, despair and lack of direction. To the new century we bring our unique gifts and offer them at the precipice.

Soulwork

Put on some soft instrumental music. Relax. Rest. In your mind's eye see yourself walking up a mountain path. Ahead is a bench. Go there and sit down. Before you is a precipice. As you gaze out over the precipice, what do you see? What hopes and possibilities arise for the future of your story and the universe's story? Sink more and more deeply

---

If the only prayer you ever say is "Thank you," that will suffice.

—Meister Eckhart

Our goal is to create a beloved community and this will require a quantitative change in our words as well as a qualitative change in our lives.

—Martin Luther King, Jr.

62

into relaxation and let your mind range freely over your hopes and dreams for the future of the planet here on this precipice of new beginnings.

When it feels right (usually as the music comes to an end), emerge from your relaxed state and write about your experience in your journal.

As midwives for a new ecological era and hospice workers for a culture about to die, we need to address two important questions: What needs to be born? What needs to die?

It is most important for those of us who want revolutionary change to understand that revolution must be preceded by reformation.

—Saul Alinsky

Cultural Violence

Pondering

Images of violence flood our culture as we stand at the precipice, imprinting themselves on the screens of our souls. This is especially evidenced in how we choose to feed our souls in our leisure and entertainment: in movies, television and sports. Just as "action" movies are often the biggest hits, the appeal of athletics seems to depend on the amount of violence in a sport. For example, the popularity of football, one of the most violent sports, is evident in the Super Bowl annually being among TV's most-watched events.

> They shall beat their swords into plowshares.
>
> —Isaiah 2: 4

Children are often schooled in this world of violence through sports programs. Boys often drop their gloves and sticks to fight in hockey games, imitating pro players whose fights are seen as crowd-pleasers and "good copy" for news stories. They likewise emulate "action heroes" in their "physical prowess." When we take into account the human conflicts depicted in the news media, we become acutely aware that we live in a culture of violence.

This deep-seated dynamic of violence demonstrates the extent of the spiritual crisis that permeates our experience. It plays itself out in our interactions with each other and our relationship to Earth. When we move from admiration to envy, from envy to resentment, from resentment to violence, we act out the dynamic of destruction. This touches the soul of our daily existence.

> Perseverance is more prevailing than violence; and many things which cannot be overcome when they are together, yield themselves up when taken little by little.
>
> —Plutarch

The challenge before us is to heal the aggression from within and rediscover a planet and people who will give birth to a renewed possibility of peace. Perhaps only when we heal our aggression toward Earth will we be able to celebrate peace on Earth as it flows out of peace *with* the Earth.

Soulwork

Violence permeates our culture. It can take many forms: domestic, civil, religious, ecological. Take a few minutes to explore the experience and implications of violence in your life.

Go to a place where destruction and violence have taken place. You may find yourself in the inner city, where people are mistreated and abused, or in a place where pollution abounds, in a toxic dump where poison and aggression against Earth is painfully present.

In silence, be present to this locus of violence. Allow this place of human pain or ecological devastation to speak to you. Observe what is there; what do you see, hear, touch, smell? What do you think?

After about ten minutes, focus your attention specifically on the pain of the people or the place where violence has occurred.

After another ten minutes, find a quiet place and record your reactions. If possible, share your experience with a friend or colleague. Reflect on how your understanding of violence has been enhanced as a result of this process.

> Violence and creativity are multivalent words having distinct meanings for the galactic periods, the stellar worlds . . . the organic and the lunar conditions.
>
> —Thomas Berry and Brian Swimme

> Do you think you can take over the universe and improve it? The universe is sacred, you cannot improve it. If you try to change it, you will ruin it. If you try to hold it, you will lose it. Achieve results, because this is the natural way. Achieve results, but not through violence.
>
> —Lao Tsu

III.

An Integral Life

The skin of deeply spiritual persons
is not a dividing membrane
that separates them from the world
but a connecting membrane, a permeable membrane,
through which events of the world
and events of their inner life
flow into one another.

—Patricia Mische

Wholistic spirituality needs to bring together science
and spirituality, religion and social justice, the psyche
and social revolution.

—Rosemary Radford Ruether

Each of us must take our place in the unfolding mystery
that is at the heart of the universe.

—Miriam MacGillis

. . . for having celebrated the lives of the uncelebrated;
for lending voice to the face in the crowd. That's what I
believe oral history is about. It's about those who shed
their tears. Or laughed during those rare moments of
triumph.

—Studs Turkel

Stories are intercessories between the fire itself and those
who would be warmed by it.

—John Shea

The Story

Pondering

My father loved stories. In his later years he would invite neighbors to join him on the front porch to tell stories. As a child I too loved stories — stories told at campfires, stories told by farmers as they looked over their land on Sunday after church. As I grew older, I began to understand that our family had a story. So did our village and county. I realized that Sunday morning was also about storytelling. Jesus was a storyteller and the Gospel a book of stories.

Stories are a prime way we communicate, the primary way humans learn. Stories shape the contours of our consciousness and alter the landscape of our souls. Stories refresh and satisfy. They are instruments of grief, healing and hope. Stories reveal who we are and what we are called to be; they express what lies deep within.

As a community organizer, I realized that within the story of a community and a people lies a primary resource for justice and change. More recently, the new science and cosmology have taught me that the universe and the Earth have a spiritual story too — that reveals and connects us to the divine. The Earth is itself a sacred story. In this story the human race is seen emerging from the physical and psychic dimensions of the Earth. Within that story are the seeds for personal and communal healing and wholeness.

An urgent challenge for our time is to dynamically integrate the Story of the Universe and the Story of Geo-Justice. Only then will we truly realize a planetary Pentecost, a world and culture of balance, harmony and peace.

Soulwork

The process of remembering our ancestors is an important vehicle for getting in touch with our personal and family story. Starting with your own name and then the names of your mother and father and grandparents, recite the names of your ancestors as far back as you can remember. Think about each of their roles in your family story. Give thanks for the forebears of your family.

> We explain things by telling their story — how they came into being and the changes that have taken place over the course of time, whether minutes or millenniums.
>
> —Thomas Berry

> My tactic has always been "Tell the Story."
>
> —Daniel Berrigan

> The heart after all is raised on a mess of stories. Then it writes its own.
>
> —Joe Wood

Celebrating Our Story

Pondering

The desire to celebrate through ritual and liturgy lies deep within the human heart. We find ways to be together, to share food and drink, to be involved in movement and touch, to reflect in silence. In transforming our everyday actions, we make possible a fully human existence; we see in eating, bathing, talking and going about our daily tasks, opportunities to deepen our lives, to see all creation as a sanctuary, to remember with gratitude our ancestors — relatives, rocks, the ocean. Our story is intimately related to Earth's story.

The Scriptures of our culture tell the wondrous story of our spiritual ancestors and of our religious roots. In viewing the "picture rocks" in Arizona, I was similarly in awe at the records and pictures on the rocks as well as the sense of history. At this precipice time of transition, we need to tell our story to remember who we are and to awaken us to who we can become. As we name and recount our spiritual journey, we connect to our family, the culture, the Earth and our God.

Soulwork

Go through a family photo album and reflect on a picture that makes you feel alive. Reflect on a book, passage or story from Scripture that speaks dynamically to your life story.

Is there an area that makes your tie to the natural world, God's creation, come alive? Perhaps the Painted Desert speaks to you, or Muir Woods in California, or the ocean breaking over the boulders off the coast of Rhode Island. Maybe you feel your story blend with the Earth's story in the rain sweeping across the fields in the Midwest, in the chirping of insects on a humid Southern night, or in the vast clean expanse of new-fallen snow. Reflect on your own experience. Then tell someone this chapter of your story.

Our hope is that the work we are doing, demanding as it is, is succeeding, and that we are on our way to a grand celebratory phase of the Earth, of life, of the human community — a new phase in the story of the universe.

—Thomas Berry

There is a world beyond ours, a world that is far away, nearby, and invisible, and it is where God lives, where the dead live, the spirit and the saints, a world where everything has already happened and everything is known. That world talks. It has a language of its own. I report what it says.

—Maria Sabina

A Story of Birth and Rebirth

Pondering

When life happens, death happens. In the instant a child is born, he or she begins to die. And when an organization begins (is born), it also begins to disintegrate and depart from its founding purpose (to die). The interplay between birth and death and the search to heal the pain of separation are at the very center of this precipice period of transition. That interplay provides a template for healing our wounded relationships with each other and also our relationship to creation.

Rebirth can happen in many ways and on many levels. It can happen when nations gather to fashion from their individual sovereignties a new world order. It can happen when employees of corporations come together to search for ways to transcend competitiveness, to share ownership and design ecological strategies. The pain of division can be healed in our churches when there is a renewed concern for the Earth and an interest in dialogue with other traditions. It can happen when we accept the many "little deaths" that make up our lives and move on to the next "birth" that is awaiting us.

One of the greatest truths of our spiritual wisdom is that there is an intrinsic logic to the unfolding of the soul, the psyche, the human journey and to the very unfolding of the universe. Having faith in the process of our unfolding is the precondition for embracing fully the transformational opportunities of our lives. History teaches us respect for our ancestors and for our own journey. The capacity to acknowledge that there is a divine wisdom and intentionality to our lives brings comfort and purpose.

Soulwork

Pray for the grace to accept the "little deaths" that are an inevitable part of your life story — the uncertainty of employment, health problems, fractured relationships with family and friends.

Ultimate meaning is embedded in story, not in facts.

—Diarmuid O'Murchu

Thus the human race passed from a rather static concept of reality to a more dynamic one. In consequence there has arisen a new series of problems, a series as important as can be, calling for new series of analysis and synthesis.

—*Gaudium et Spes*
Vatican II (par. #5)

Take time today to honor the unfolding of your life and to celebrate life's epiphanies — communication at a family meal, tucking in your child at bedtime, the wonder of a sunrise, a dream that clarifies an ambiguity and clearly speaks the language of the divine.

See in these deaths and life-gifts the circle of death and rebirth that is part of the universe's story.

How does the New Story challenge us to engage the following transformations:

- ◆ Consciousness — to see all of life as evolutionary and unfolding.
- ◆ Technology — as placed in the service of Earth and its peoples rather than for subjegation, oppression and devastation.
- ◆ To see the New Story as a vehicle of Geo-Justice by restructuring relationships toward balance, harmony and peace.

Blessed be you, mighty matter, irresistible march of evolution, reality ever new born; you who, by constantly shattering our mental categories, force us to go ever further and further in our pursuit of the truth.

—Teilhard de Chardin

Journey of the Soul

Pondering

The spiritual journey challenges us to be willing to look closely at moments of transition. To embrace these moments requires a willingness to surrender to the death of our ego and to be open to what John of the Cross called the "dark night of the soul."

As we enter fully into the process, traveling into the "dark night," we are required to let go of control and surrender to the deeper currents of life that emerge from the events of our day and the depths of our innermost self.

Encouraged and strengthened in this process, we learn to let go. We realize that much in life is beyond our control, and we acknowledge this reality as we sink into both the limits and the possibilities of life. As we deepen the experience of this process, we come to know a new level of freedom.

This freedom will be achieved by a threefold process. Initially we will gain the capacity to divert our minds from circular thinking and preoccupation with uncontrollable elements of our lives. The second phase involves letting go and surrendering the outcome of our concerns to the graciousness of the Divine. The concluding phase involves engaging in life.

The outcome of this journey is an increased trust in the Divine and a capacity to think creatively in a new manner. The hoped-for result will be a life of wisdom, creativity and compassion that moves us beyond the precipice.[3]

Soulwork

The spiritual journey involves working toward bringing our lives into greater harmony with the dynamics of the universe and the internal trajectory of our lives. The process involves a few basic principles:

♦ Empty your mind of preoccupations or distractions.

> Wisdom is ofttimes
>   nearer when we stoop
> Than when we soar.
>
> —William Wordsworth,
>   "The Excursions"

> We are like flies crawling across the Sistine Chapel. We cannot see what angels and gods lie underneath the threshold of our perceptions. We do not live in reality; we live in our paradigms, our historical perceptions, our illusions. We share through culture what we call reality, but the true reality of our condition is invisible.
>
> —William Irwin
>   Thompson

71

◆ Listen to inner currents (of the Spirit).

◆ Realizing that you do not control the many factors that impinge upon your life, let go of the illusion of control and reflect on your realization that the cosmos and your life are in the mind of the Divine.

◆ Focus your energies on the aspects of your life that you *can* affect; put every effort possible into the things that you *can* change.

◆ At all stages in the process, strive to achieve an increased consciousness of your own story and realize that others have their own unique destinies and directions.

◆ Take time each day with the natural world as you ponder your life's direction and become open to the wisdom and insights revealed through your presence in creation.

The Call

Pondering

Some have described today's society as a culture without vocation. As a people, we are without a deep sense of purpose, identity or destiny. Many things contribute to this. Young people often have little confidence in the future. Employment opportunities are limited, and many people are forced to settle for low-paying jobs without much hope for challenging work or advancement. At the same time, advertising emphasizes immediate gratification. And why not, since life seems temporary and unsure? This view of life, in turn, further militates against commitment to long-term career preparation and goals that require delayed gratification.

> If your project is smaller than your lifetime you've got no ambition.
>
> —I.F. Stone

In an era of turbulence and transition, alienation abounds; people feel disconnected from family, themselves and Earth. Our sense of homelessness echoes our primary "homelessness" from the Earth.

Everywhere I go I sense the hunger for a calling, a vocation. People experience a deep desire to be in touch with the Mystery that continues to call us into life — whether they can articulate their longing clearly or not.

> Go confidently in the direction of your dreams. Live the life you've imagined.
>
> —Henry David Thoreau

My own deepest desire always has been to be who I am supposed to be; I want to live my life for the purpose it was intended and to embrace the ambiguity of choice. I want to acknowledge that there is no certitude, yet live conditionally as if there were. I want to live fully, with generosity and gratitude, and to break new ground, not always follow the paths of others.

> If I never become who I'm supposed to be I will spend the rest of my life contradicting myself, Being neither who I am Or who I could become.
>
> —Thomas Merton

Soulwork

Galway Bay, the "wearin' o' the green," the phrase *Erin go bragh*, the shamrock — all are symbols for the Irish, or more specifically, for St. Patrick's Day. They remind those of us of Irish descent to remember our past and celebrate our present.

Think about the symbols of your cultural heritage.

These symbols are a rich heritage, a particular path by which you are called to celebrate the divine. Spend time today thinking about the connections between your heritage and the practice of your faith.

And if you are of mixed or uncertain cultural heritage, celebrate the wonder of diversity in creation and in your life.

God does not ask anything else of you except that you let yourself go and let God
be God
in you.

—Meister Eckhart

The Life of an Institution

Pondering

While a student at the Industrial Areas Foundation Saul Alinsky Training Institute, I learned that five to eight years after the beginning of an organization it will predictably grow to oppose the very purpose for which it was created.

There is a lot of practical evidence of this principle. Political candidates campaign to change the world and then spend their time in office fund-raising for reelection. Academics dedicate long years of study to the pursuit of wisdom and truth, and then spend their teaching years maneuvering for tenure and endowed chairs and grants. Business people strive to find more and better ways to serve humanity and Earth and then succumb to the pressures of the "bottom line," resume-building and the desire to increase their retirement benefits. Religious leaders enter the ministry in response to a vocational call and then find themselves playing hierarchical politics and working to support structures that are hardly examples of the Gospel in action.

The challenge for all of us in our personal and professional lives is to bring forth new life from dying structures. Sometimes that means letting go of projects and programs that have outlived their time.

Soulwork

Institutions fall into four broad categories: religious, business, political and educational. Think about how you associate with each type of institution in your life.

What are your memories and experiences? For example, as a child, how did you relate to the church? Now, as an adult, how do you see yourself in relation to religion? In the political arena, where do you see yourself on the continuum — left? right? center? Do you support technology in the choices you make? How do you relate to the corporate world? Is your job in big business? What motivates you? How have your attitudes about various institutions changed over the years? Have they changed? *Should*

We're all assigned a piece of garden, a corner of the universe that is ours to transform. Our corner of the universe is our own life — our relationships, our homes, our work, our current circumstances — exactly as they are.

—Marianne Williamson

Rediscover our role as co-creators with God, participants in the transformation of the world into the new heaven and the new earth.

—Diarmuid O'Marchu

I should like to love my country and still have justice.

—Camus

75

they change? Have the institutions changed? Do you have a part to play in changing them?

After reflecting on each aspect of institutions, ask yourself what is life-giving in the institutions in your life. Then, think about ways *you* may need to change in order to relate to the structures in your life.

Organizations of all stripes are known for renewals of what might better be thrown overboard. Committees labor intensely to freshen up worn-out procedures, redecorate the obsolete and remodel what should not be done at all. Yet there is hope that the new millennium may see truly creative committees, collaborative teams of what Walt Disney called "imagineers," committees that are given the freedom to image and create something new and innovative. Many are the aging and stuffy institutions that could benefit from such a creative committee of imagineers.

—Edward Hays

To Be Human

Pondering

Living a human life in this time of transition is a challenging responsibility and task. We are *Homo sapiens*, the "wise and rational animal." Today we are called to revise that definition. In fact, some have suggested that our task is to "reinvent the human" — to understand our relationship to self, others and the other-than-human world differently. This new relationship will mean thinking differently about our life-model and dreaming differently about how the world could be.

While studying chemistry in college, I worked in Canada's largest industrial research laboratory. The long-term effects of the pesticides and fertilizers with which I worked did not concern me at that time. I did not know that the petrochemical industry was at that time — and would continue — playing havoc with the health of the planet. I did not realize the significance of the dysfunction in the human-Earth relationship. The oil slick on the river and erosion of the ice in winter were early warning signs of what we face today. But I didn't think much about them.

Many issues failed to affect me then — the oppression of women, minorities, indigenous peoples, and the oppression of Earth itself. They affect me now. Indeed, I believe that to be human demands that they be important and that the oppressed be free.

Soulwork

Co-creation happens when we are connected to our deepest self. It is a process that is liberating, decisive and clear. To co-create involves living with the intention of being responsible, committed, and at the service of whatever calls to us. Co-creative action flows out of our vision of life, ourselves, Earth and the divine.

What is your vision? After reflecting on it today (and perhaps tomorrow, and the next day . . .), express your vision in a concrete form that has meaning for you. This could be

> We forget too easily what miracles we are! At our best we're like bubbling, brave, dazzling comets. No wonder God loves us! I confess to delight in full-bodied, juicy, quirky people, because they seem working definitions of what it means to be saintly, whole, responsibly free — to be truly human.
>
> —Rich Heffern

> The human is a threshold person.
>
> —John O'Donohue

a written description, a poem, a drawing, a photograph, a song. It may be something you create yourself or something you find that resonates with your inner view of what your life is all about. Keep this concrete reminder of your vision close to you so that it will remind you daily of who you are and what you are about — and be always ready to revise your vision.

Without a dream, the people perish.

—Proverbs 29: 18

The glory of God is a human fully alive.

—Irenaeus of Lyons

Integrity and Truth

Pondering

Perhaps the greatest insult we can feel is being accused of lying. Most of us are insulted when our integrity is questioned in the slightest way — whether it is verifying a check, questioning our account of an incident or doubting the accuracy of our memory. We experience a deep sense of rejection when questioned about our truthfulness. It is as if our very *being* is somehow called into question and found wanting.

Yet sometimes we fail to be completely truthful with ourselves. A spirituality of truth and integrity means being fully who we are, being in full communion with ourselves. Robert Muller names well the call to integrity and truth in our time when he writes: "Humanity is ready for a new culture. That culture must include the benefits derived from solitude, meditation, prayer and spirituality right in the middle of daily action and life."

Soulwork

Take some time to do the hard work of asking yourself how closely your inner convictions correspond to your actions in the world, including how you are using your gifts. To what degree are denial or false consciousness factors that contribute to incongruity in your life? To what extent are there contradictions in your life? In what way do you plan to create greater congruence between what you say and what you do?

Reflect on how your interiority can foster and support increased coherence in your life and lifestyle.

No legacy is so rich as honesty.

—Shakespeare

Each thing: Each stone, blossom, child is held in place.

—Reike

Our consciousness has the character of unbroken wholeness. It hangs together and allows our experience to do so.

—Danah Zohar

79

The Call to Congruence

Pondering

The call to congruence is the call to live in harmony with the deepest, most integral part of ourselves and to live in balance with Earth. It is the call to discover a deep resonance between the impulses and vibrations of our own existence and the aspirations of our lives. As humans, we have a deep appetite for joy; our hearts yearn for it. We are ever looking for a story that we can embrace — a new story, a deepening story — one that resonates with what we intuit to be true.

While immersed in pathology and pathos, we long to live functionally on the Earth. We dream of a culture whose images and language reveal our origins and how we are to proceed through time as we look forward toward the future, whether "minutes or millennia."

Where do we begin? What opens us to the inner and outer congruence that brings us joy in life? Simply, we need to learn the story: the New Story of our origins inherent in our Scriptures and ancient myths. This story is further revealed by science and the transformational events that have marked our beginning and how we have arrived at where we are today.

This story is ongoing; it will continue to be modified as new data becomes known. But more important than its scientific accuracy is its sacredness. As a basis and organizing principle of a new literacy and intimacy with creation, the New Story is an ongoing source of revelation that casts some light into the darkness we face from our cultural precipice.

Awakening to the New Story can help us rediscover the sacredness and depths of life. In this way, relating to the world around us becomes a spiritual experience: eating a raspberry in our backyard, looking across a meadow to a creek, standing on the shore of a river. Such simple yet charged moments can remind us of our childhood, activate our recollections of the universe's fifteen-billion-year history and connect us to the divine. As we revisit our memories

---

If you do not have the eyes to see the divine image in all things, you do not have the eyes to see the divine image in anything.

—Richard Rohr

The stories you tell one
another around
fires in the dark
Will make you strong
and wise.

—Alla Rene Bozarth

We look before and after,
And pine for what is not;
Our sincerest laughter
With some pain is fraught;
Our sweetest songs are
those that tell of saddest
thought.

—Percy Bysshe Shelley,
"To a Skylark"

---

and our times of oneness with the universe and God, we realize these experiences as moments of grace.

Looking at these experiences through the language and legacy of our traditions requires trust, patience and a capacity for ambiguity. Looking at my childhood and the evolution of my spiritual journey, there are three aspects of my Christian tradition that particularly have provided continuity and bridges in this time of accelerated cultural change and disbelief. They are the sacramentality of life, the paschal mystery and the trinitarian dimension of all existence. These aspects continue to be lenses of a living faith. As we make connections and ground our experience in the touchstones of our tradition, we view the New Story, the universe, the Earth, and every dimension of life on it, as sacred and revelatory.

Only by exploring our deepest feelings honestly will we enter into a realm of forgiveness, harmony and profound peace. By uncapping our feelings and emotions we can be cleansed and become open and vulnerable, in touch with our true needs. And by honoring our needs we grow in compassion toward others, Earth — and ourselves.

Soulwork

The call to congruence is a call to resonate with and connect to the deepest ground of our being, to the inner child. It is that part of ourselves that is whole, that relates directly, without pretense or excessive self-consciousness, to the world and the people around us, that has a clear relationship to earth and sky.

We need to work to revive and heal our inner child. To help you get in touch with the child inside, draw a picture or find a photograph of yourself as a child and post it on your refrigerator as a reminder that now, as an adult, you can love and nourish that child.

As you look at the picture, decide on one concrete action you can take this week in that child's behalf.

I wish from now on to be the first to become conscious of all that the world loves, pursues, and suffers; I want to be the first to seek, to sympathize, and to suffer; the first to unfold and sacrifice myself — to become more widely human and more nobly of the earth than any of the world's servants.

—Teilhard de Chardin

Some day we will regard our children not as creatures to manipulate or change but as messengers from a world we once deeply knew but which we have long since forgotten.

—Alice Miller

81

The Signature of the Divine

Pondering

During February, at about 5 P.M., as dusk was settling in, Aunt Margaret would stand at the window and proclaim: "The days are getting longer." After the burden of winter, the longer days were a promise that spring would eventually arrive.

Recently I asked a group of children, "How do you feel about darkness and light?" One boy said he liked the darkness because he "could go into the basement and rollerblade." A roar of laughter from the listening adults and children bounced across the room.

My second question was, "Do any of you appreciate the light?" "I do," the same boy answered, "because I have my flashlight with me when I'm rollerblading in the basement." This time the laughter was twice as loud!

Still, his responses to the dark and light reaffirmed the fascination and engagement that all of us have with the dynamic that reveals the paschal mystery aspect of reality — the life, death and resurrection cycle that permeates all of life. Darkness often manifests when we, as a people and a culture, tend to isolate and fixate on particular issues; when this happens, we lose the larger context and interconnectedness of all things. We surrender our narrow perspective as we strive for a "seamless garment" and for "common ground." Saul Alinsky, radical and architect of community organization, spoke to this when he said, "The question is not is there life after death, but is there life after birth?"

The struggle with the forces of darkness are evident in our lives today. Most Western governments practice a global economy based on competition and exploitation, favoring the rich and overburdening the poor. The splintering of "church people" into different camps that fixate on particular questions of justice and/or morality leads to potentially harmful divisions within churches.

We are called to become a culture of relationships rather than a culture of law. Life-giving threads emanate

> One might say that a hitherto unknown form of religion — one that no one could as yet have imagined or described, for a lack of a universe large enough and organic enough to contain it, is burgeoning in the heart of modern man, from a seed sown by the idea of evolution.... Far from being shaken in my faith by such a revolution, it is with irrepressible hope that I welcome the irresistible rise of this new mysticism and anticipate its equally inevitable triumph.
>
> —Teilhard de Chardin

82

from sources like the New Story and process theology —
moving us toward the new millennium and beyond in a new
web of connectedness that is the signature of the divine. If
nurtured, this web can astonish us with support and continually energize us with new hope.

As we stand at the precipice, we are asked to take up
the challenge to become "trinitarian people" — people who
understand and celebrate *uniqueness*, *diversity* and *communion*. We honor oneness and multiplicity within the web of
creation. We honor the soul of every person, tree, animal
and other expression of God's creation. In the uniqueness of
every part of creation we discover and are energized by the
spark of the divine Spirit. When we celebrate diversity,
perhaps of race, gender or sexual orientation, we honor the
spiritual breadth of all creation. When we celebrate communion, we recognize that there is no evidence of separation
within the community of life.

Soulwork

Take time today to examine and celebrate diversity.
For example, reflect on your family members and marvel at
how unique each is. Or pick up two leaves from the same
tree and discover how different they are. Or share a conversation with someone with a different racial or class background. See how your life is enriched by the diversity that
surrounds you.

Wisdom calls aloud in the streets. She raises her voice in the public squares. She calls out at the street corners. She delivers her message at the city gates.

—Proverbs 1: 20-21

Our task must be to free ourselves from this prison by widening our circle of compassion to embrace all living creatures and the whole of nature in its beauty.

—Albert Einstein

Re-Enchantment

Pondering

Michael Lerner, in *The Politics of Meaning*, indicates that the crises of materialism and cynicism have flooded our culture because of a lack of meaning and purpose in our lives. Thomas Moore, particularly in *The Re-Enchantment of Everyday Life*, takes us another step and reminds us of the need for magic, beauty and enchantment in our lives. It is then that we become alive from the inside, experience the "exaltation of existence," where every cell comes alive as we experience the embrace of, and oneness with, all creation.

Re-enchantment makes possible a sense of the sacred, the savoring of each moment, each person, each member of the Earth community. As we look out from the precipice into a world of enchantment, we discover a new sense of balance, harmony and peace with each aspect of creation understood as an expression of the divine.

Our spirituality is a vehicle toward meaning — and enchantment. But shifting to a new mode of consciousness, one precipitated by the new millennium, requires seeing the world differently. For example, on a construction site you might ask workers, "What are you doing?" Answers could range from "laying brick" to "supporting my family" to "building a house for God." These different ways of seeing the world reflect an increasingly expansive perspective.

In a sense re-enchantment involves answering life's questions from a wondrous and spiritual perspective. It is about welcoming each moment of life as a time of amazing grace. Jonathan Kozol, in his book on the lives of children, *Amazing Grace*, tells about a thirteen-year-old boy in the Bronx. He asked the boy what he thought the world would be like if people lived their spirituality. Later the boy gave him a paper: "In a truly spiritual world there would be no crack; homes would be without violence; every child would have two parents; every father would have a job; the streets would be safe; and God would be fond of everyone."

True spirituality celebrates each moment as precious,

each person as sacred, each aspect of creation as a reflection of the divine.

Soulwork

Take a small step today toward bringing enchantment into your life. Reflect upon Kozol's question: What would the world be like if people lived their spirituality? Ask yourself how your world would be changed if your spirituality were alive with enchantment and if you truly lived your spirituality. How can you move toward that "enchanted" world?

Whoever loves wisdom loves life.

—Sirach 4: 12

Sacred Earth,
With gratitude and grace
We celebrate the story
Of creation, liberation,
    and us.
In blessing and
    brokenness
We restore hunger for
    newness
Boiling from the
    wellsprings of our souls.
Here within wonder
    and surprise
We rediscover hope
And recognize once more
    the signature of God

Remembering

Pondering

I remember how much my mother wanted my sister to have our grandmother's ring and bracelet. They were more than decorative pieces; they were mementos of a family heritage, a way of making the past present. Today they continue to evoke memories, and my niece now wears the bracelet.

I treasure two gifts that remind me of a special trip, but that also contain genetic memories of the past. One is a St. Brigid's Cross, cut from reeds in an Irish field; the other is a shillelagh, cut from a tree on the adjoining farmland in County Armaugh in Ireland, the home of my ancestors.

From a liturgical perspective, one of the highlight remembrances of my life came in the hills of Kentucky, at Gethsemani Abbey, then the home of Thomas Merton. To celebrate the feast of Corpus Christi, monks and visitors alike processed through the cloister of the monastery. All along the floor were streams of flowers. This walkway of beauty was prepared to remind us of the mystery of the Christian liturgy.

My Gethsemani story reminded a friend of a similar event when she was in Germany. The entire village had prepared flowers and a procession. Sharing our stories helps trigger others' memories, as well as helping us key into our collective story.

Memories are important; we do well to take time to celebrate them. When we do, we honor our roots, connect to our ancestors and make present the richness of the past.

Remembering and celebrating are important spiritual practices that enrich the present and help the future flourish from the roots grounded in our past.

Soulwork

Close your eyes. Stand quietly (or imagine doing so) in the center of a dimly lit room. (Lighted candles provide a good ambience.) Take a step backward,[4] and imagine that you are your same-sex parent. Allow your memories of

Isn't all poetry a way of remembering? Poets gather, as Rilke saw it, the nectar of the visible into the great honeycomb of the invisible.

—Br. David Steindl-Rast, OSB

Celebration and remembrance form the life-giving center of our spirituality.

—Edward Hays

Memories ripen like winter apples on the shelf.

—Br. David Steindl-Rast, OSB

86

family stories to come tumbling into your consciousness. Try to experience them as your parent did.

Take another step backward and repeat the process with memories of and about your same-sex grandparent.

Step back and repeat the process with memories of your great-grandparent.

Then step forward, slowly through each generation, feeling the "person" of each ancestor.

Consider writing your recollections and your feelings in your journal.

Or, take an inventory of your home and study how the reminders that surround you reveal who you are. You may want to create a particular area in your home to display "treasures" and family mementos that are part of your life's journey. For example, in my apartment I have:

♦ an icon of Martin Luther King, Jr., along with pins, bookmarks and candles. This "altar" reminds me of this modern-day prophet and my appreciation for his work for peace through racial and economic justice.

♦ pictures of baseball teams I have played for; the plaque announcing my induction into the Sports Hall of Fame in Sarnia/Lambton County; my glove; books about baseball. These souvenirs remind me of how this game was for me — and in some ways still is — a source of wisdom, a "way of life."

♦ pictures of my parents, brother and sister; a plaque of my Irish ancestors; clumps of "bioregional earth" from the farms and graves of my Irish and French ancestors in Canada and Ireland. These remind me of my roots and the earth from where I've come.

This is the use of memory: for liberation.

—T.S. Eliot

Recollections

Perspectives on the
    past
Summon hope and
    possibility
Toward life's unfold-
    ing path.
Former adventures of
    the cosmos
Tell of their search
For a world of affirma-
    tion
Midst the muddiness
    of life.
Summoned by a new
    perspective
We recall
That others have
    walked this road
Of turbulence and
    truth.
From this cradle of the
    cosmos
The courage of the past
Reminds us, once again,
Of the pulsating
    emergence of
    new life.

Meaning and Simplicity

Pondering

I used to wonder how a four-year-old could become so caught up in the consumer world of fast food and toys. But I see that the media — and lots of adults with the same message — teach children that well-being is achieved when we buy and consume. Toys like the Power Rangers and movies like *Pocahontas* and *Hercules*, with all their spin-off products, manipulate the psyche, forming it with a certain view of what it means to be fulfilled and realized as a human.

As adults we continue "buying well to live well." Deep in the cultural coding is a conviction that buying and consuming will heal our pain and make us whole. The "American Dream" is an economic gospel that proclaims "more is better" and promises that fast and unlimited growth in terms of production, distribution and consumption is the key to realizing our greatest potential.

This view flourishes on Wall Street and Bay Street — and probably even on your street. Yet there is a growing suspicion that the meaning and purpose of life cannot be achieved merely by acquiring more and more things. Many of us have come to realize that the desire for products is, in fact, a misguided mysticism. "How much money is enough?" someone once asked Henry Ford. His answer, "One more dollar," shows the inadequacy of the material to substitute for the divine.

As a result of this awareness of the inadequacies of materialism's promises, many of us are starting to simplify our lifestyles, buying and using less, perhaps even moving from the suburbs to a city or farm. We feel the growing need to attune our lifestyle to the rhythms of the planet. We are also becoming more ecologically aware and more sensitive to the pain and needs of the Earth, as well as those of the poor and marginalized.

This increased awareness leads us to want to build a world of greater meaning and purpose, of increased love,

> I went to the woods because I wished to live deliberately, to front only the essential facts of life, and see if I could not learn what it had to teach.
>
> —Henry David Thoreau

> The Buddhist sees that the essence of civilization is not in a multiplication of wants but in a purification of human character.
>
> —E. F. Schumacher

caring and respect. No longer do we see society as a world of products and people to be bought and sold by consumer relationships. We long to bring about a new world of peace and plenty for all, which is, after all, what Jesus described as the reign of God.

Soulwork

In consumer-oriented and wealthy countries like the United States and Canada, many people use more than their fair share of Earth's resources. Yet Americans are also a generous people, quick to respond to the needs generated by natural disasters. The problem is that too often we simply don't notice the less dramatic but equally painful needs that permeate the lives of the poor and marginalized among us. We don't *see* the poor — and therefore we do nothing for them.

Today, now, identify one area in which your consumption is higher than it needs to be. In addition to resolving to cut back in that area, put in motion a concrete plan for transferring what you save to someone who is in need.

How could anyone ever tell you you were anything less than beautiful?

—Shaina Noll

Most of the luxuries, and many of the so-called comforts of life, are not only not indispensable but positive hindrances to our elevation.

—Henry David Thoreau

89

IV.

Beginning Again, and Until . . .

*To be of the Earth is to know the restlessness of being a seed,
the darkness of being planted, the struggle toward the light,
the pain of growth into the light, the joy of bursting and
        bearing fruit,
the love of being food for someone, the scattering
        of your seeds,
the decay of the seasons, the mystery of death,
        and the miracle of birth.*

—John Soos

*God is a circle whose circumference is here and whose
center is everywhere.*

—Hindu Scripture

*He will never waver,
        nor be crushed
Until true justice is
        established on Earth.*

—Isaiah 42: 4

90

Finding Our Way Home

Pondering

We are at the threshold of something extremely exciting. We are also at the end of something. It's like watching a trapeze artist at work. She swings out, holding onto the bar, and then lets go with the expectation that there will be something there to catch on to. I think most of us are "over the net." We have to let go of the old paradigm in expectation of the new.

We are coming to the end of the industrial age. The question is: How do we find our place on the planet at this point in history? One way, I believe, lies in recognizing where we are wounded. My childhood, for example, was disrupted by my mother's illness. As an adult I tried to heal myself of my childhood pain by healing others. I believe that if we research our pain we'll find our avenues of energy. It's not the only way, but it's one. Henri Nouwen says:

> [We need] to recognize the sufferings of the times in our own heart and make that recognition the starting point of service. To enter into a dislocated world. Relating to a compulsive generation will not be perceived as authentic unless it comes from the heart — wounded by the suffering about you that you see.

Being at home with our wounds is integral to being generative and life-producing in the world.

Another way of finding our place on the planet is through homecoming. Home is where everything begins. Wendell Berry, Kentucky farmer and poet, writes:

> The world can't be discovered by a journey of miles, no matter how long. Only by a spiritual journey — a journey very arduous and humble and joyful by which we arrive at the ground at our feet, where we learn to be at home.

We are on a journey that has already begun. To know

If you really want something badly enough you've got to let it go free. And if it comes back to you it's really yours. If it doesn't you never had it anyway.

—Goethe's *Kitchen*

The earth is our house and a place of mystery and God's handiwork.

—George Washington Carver

It is only by coming home to ourselves that we can survive.

—Susan Griffin

---

that we are not alone on this journey is important. To keep moving is also important because, believe it or not, we can get stuck in pleasure, or pain (which we probably have more practice in), or creativity (which most of us would probably like to do) or even in justice. Yet justice has become an abstraction in our culture — a "how to" and an "ought to" — not a joyful undertaking. We need to help each other on the journey by being soul-mates, fellow-travelers.

Dag Hammarskjold writes:

> I don't know who or what put the question. I don't even know when it was put. I don't even remember answering. But at some moment I did answer yes to someone or to something. And from that hour I was certain that existence was meaningful and therefore my life was self-surrendered and whole.

Soulwork

Reflect on one of the two ways of finding your place discussed above: woundedness or homecoming.

Woundedness — Think about your childhood. Do you have any memories that cause you pain? How is that pain affecting your life now?

Homecoming — Try to recall a recent event, person or place that made you feel "at home." What caused the feeling? How did you react?

There is no house like the house of belonging.

—David Whyte

Does one really have to fret about enlightenment? No matter what road I travel I'm going home.

—Shinsho

Welcoming the Outsider

Pondering

Years ago I was on an urban plunge in Toronto's inner city, an experience designed to assist participants to see, in a new way, the poor and homeless of Canada's largest city.

Now I live in Berkeley, California, a city known as the birthplace of political movements fostered on the campus of the University of California. It is a city for the "outsider"; Berkeley welcomes diversity. But it is also a lonely city. Its streets are crowded with displaced persons who are "poor, passed by and possessed" by a city known for People's Park and the Free Speech Movement.

> You shall not violate the right of an outsider or an orphan.
>
> —Deuteronomy 24: 17

One of the outsiders is Tim, affectionately known by many as Berkeley's "Mayor of the Streets." He spends his days in front of the Claremont Coffee Shop and his nights in an open garage a few blocks away. Often I see him reading novels or the newspaper and talking with other street people. When we speak, he often says, "I have to get inside" [get an apartment]. But he never does. He's afraid of the conflicts that may arise — a possible confrontation with a landlord, too much noise from other tenants, loss of freedom. He remains in the garage, his shelter from the night, and muses each day about his pain and his plight.

> Our friends are given to us from elsewhere.... All friendship is an experience of belonging.
>
> —John O'Donohue

Gustavo Gutiérrez, the father of liberation theology, reminds us that the divine is most present in the places of the poor. Wherever the Tims are, wherever an aspect of the Earth lies neglected or abused, there God is most present. But seeking God in such places can be dangerous. Bishop Jacques Gaillot of France was removed from his diocese because he chose to embrace the outsider, the "surplus people," those with AIDS, those who are gay, lesbian, addicted or aged. Gaillot writes:

> Christianity does not ask us to live in the shadow of the cross but in the fire of its creative action.
>
> —Teilhard de Chardin

> I had a dream to be able to accompany the poor, the excluded, the ignored without having to explain myself to the rich, the secure, or the comfortable. To be able to go where distress calls me without having to give advance notice. To

be able to show my indignation at destitution, injustice, violence, the role of weapons and managed famines without being considered a meddler in politics.... I dreamed of the freedom to think and express myself, to debate and criticize without fear of the guillotine.

Soulwork

Recognize and welcome the divine presence in the poor by making an appointment with a soup kitchen or shelter and assisting in preparing and serving a meal to the homeless of your city. Or visit an AIDS center or women's shelter and talk to the people there.

Extend your awareness by planning a "day in the green" (an "eco-plunge"). Volunteer to clean up a section along the highway or in a neighborhood park.

Reflect on your experiences in your journal.

We may well expect the same results in our life as Bishop Gaillot encountered. As prophets, if we take the Gospel seriously, we can expect to be in trouble and to be outraged. The challenge for each of us is to ponder and to decide; then we will be supported by new and fresh energy that will carry us into a new era that awaits us.

Once Dorothy Day was given a beautiful and expensive diamond ring. A little later she gave the ring to a woman who was weather-beaten, addicted, homeless. Dorothy's colleagues pointed out that the ring could have been sold and the money used to pay the woman's rent for many months to come. Dorothy's response was that the woman could do what she chose with the ring — sell it, or maybe just wear it because it was beautiful. "Do you suppose," Dorothy asked, "that God intended diamonds only for the rich?"

Singing the Song of Nature

Pondering

Concern with ecology is relatively recent in the world of culture and spirituality. *Ecology* was not in the common vocabulary when I was in college. But the ravages of the industrial age have now been impressed upon the human conscience in the form of a new awareness about our interrelatedness with all creation.

Ecology speaks of the "web of life"; it reminds us that each action, each breath, is connected to everything else. Ecology is how we look at our interrelated world. Our trinitarian God — unity in diversity, one in three — shows us how unity and diversity can dance together. Thus ecology reminds us that all life is a unique expression of the divine. In its most profound sense it is about our home and our responsibility for the habitat of others. It is about relationship, interaction and dialogue. Leonardo Boff, the liberation theologian, describes ecology as "the science and art of relationship and related beings." Integral ecology heals us of our alienation and loneliness and brings us closer to a relationship with all of life.

This grand show is eternal. It is always sunrise somewhere; the dew is never all dried at once; a shower is forever falling; vapor is ever rising. Eternal sunrise, eternal sunset, eternal dawn and gloaming, on sea and continents and islands, each in its turn, as the round earth rolls.

—John Muir

Soulwork

You as an individual are part of the web of life. To help see your life in the larger context of the Earth community, consciously network with your neighbors — write letters, make phone calls, join movements or otherwise realize your interrelatedness.

Spend time today reflecting on some of the immediate links that connect you to the web of life: To whom or what are you joined? How does that communion affect you in your everyday life? How does it influence your values, attitudes, judgments?

Eternal God, we thank you for the gift of life, wonder beyond words, our awareness of Soul, the light within, the world around us so filled with beauty, and the richness of the Earth, which day by day sustains us. For all these gifts and more we thank and bless you, the Source of All.

—Jewish Grace

Literacy for Life

Pondering

We gathered on Prince Edward Island, Canada's least populated province, around the theme of "Greening Our Isle: Geo-Justice and the Environment." Business people, farmers, educators and fishermen participated; so did people representing the government and churches.

We came together out of love for the island and a deep concern for it and its peoples.

Pesticides are being pumped into the potato crops as agribusiness demands higher production levels. The runoff from heavy rains washes into fish ponds, killing thousands of fish. Not only has the pesticide affected the crops and fish, it has also affected the health of the people living on the island.

We stand today at a moment of great peril and possibility. Prince Edward Island is a microcosm of the planet. This place of potatoes, fish and people is ill. The alarm sounded by Rachel Carson more than thirty years ago[5] is calling even more loudly to protect and foster life on this island, a place where illiteracy and unemployment dominate the lives of the people.

At this time of pain, we are being called to respond with a new "literacy for life." Basically, literacy means that we:

- ◆ cultivate a greater awareness of the disenfranchised and marginalized of the Earth;
- ◆ become fluent in the language of creation;
- ◆ awaken to what is happening to the Earth and do something about it;
- ◆ experience the pain of the wounded and toxic land and choose ways that enable the Earth to regain its health and wholeness;
- ◆ are again enchanted by the beauty that envelops our home and nourishes our soul;
- ◆ become attuned to the exhilaration of the seasons;

In contemplation the human spirit learns to see the presence of the divine in nature, and so recognizes that the Earth is a sacred place. For such a spirit the biblical bush burns, and we take off our shoes.

—Elizabeth Johnson

A new sense of literacy is needed . . . the capacity to read the Great Book of the Universe but particularly the ability to read the Book of Nature as this is presented to us in the local settings of our lives

—Thomas Berry

96

- learn to celebrate the sacred moments of our journey from birth to death;
- commit ourselves to living a life of voluntary simplicity.

Soulwork

Go to a quiet and secluded area close to your home. Spend some time walking through the area in solitude. Find a place to recline. Spend some time becoming aware of your emotional state. Take an inventory of your feelings: fear, anger, love, longing . . . . Write down your impressions, or you might even pick some member of the Earth community to dialogue with about your emotional state: a tree, meadow, brook or other inhabitant of the natural world. Take plenty of time and enter fully into the experience. If possible, share the experience with another person or a group. Or record your reflections in your journal.

You will learn more in the woods than you will in books. The trees and the stones will teach you what you will never learn at the school of the masters.

—St. Bernard

Learning: Silent Reading and Art

Pondering

We sat around the kitchen table, surrounded by dear friends in a home in the west end of Toronto, Canada's largest city. The conversation turned to education.

Joining her parents and brother, Julian, at the table was Laura. A wonderfully imaginative and creative person, Laura was not in a very positive mood about school and its impact on her life. In fact, in an earlier conversation with her mother she reported that she had received a barely passing mark from her teacher. The painful report she made to her mother brought tears to both their eyes. "That's not a bad mark for someone like me."

As the conversation continued around the table, I posed a question to Laura, "What are your favorite subjects?"

"Silent reading and art" was the response. I began to realize as I reflected on her answer that what Laura loved about learning was how she could use her imagination, the times she could read and paint and let her mind flourish and flow.

For the most part, education does not relate to the Lauras of this world. Rather than fostering a relationship with one's deepest self and with the mythic narrative informed by the new science, contemporary education prepares people to dominate Earth and all life on it through government, commerce and other areas of work. In the process we have lost our spiritual moorings at the heart of true education. Our formal learning is no longer motivated by a desire for deep meaning and purpose. We also need to have learning energized by the exultation of being alive.

Such education is characterized by a quest for "intimacy with the natural world," the capacity to "listen to the voices" and "create a context for gratitude and praise."

On several occasions I have invited participants to form three groups around the topics mentioned above. In every case the results have been profound and encouraging. On one occasion several of us reclined on the grass while

Nature is the most intimate expression of the divine imagination.

—John O'Donohue

Words are the last resort for what lies deep within.

—Rainer Maria Rilke

Let the beauty we love
Be what we do.
There are hundreds of
 ways
To kiss the ground.

—Rumi

one person read St. Francis' prayer to Brother Sun and Sister Moon. The spirit of the prayer led us to remember and reflect on moments of intimate encounter with the divine, times of connection to God through the primary sacrament of creation.

The St. Clair River spoke to me as a child; it was a poultice for my soul, refreshing, stern, entrancing and strong. It was in its presence that I began to understand life, death and rebirth, incarnation, letting go and surprise. It was at the feet of the river that I began to glimpse the meaning of life — mystical moments of depth, differentiation and interconnectedness. The river was, and is, my companion, mentor and guide; it continues to stress and celebrate the contours of my soul and is my teacher of joy and gratitude for the continuous flow of all that is and will be.

Soulwork

Go back to the days of your childhood. Recall your early intimate connections with the natural world: fields, streams or creeks, a favorite tree . . . . Reflect on what life lessons you learned in your favorite natural environment, your favorite childhood "spot." In those places and times did you experience or cultivate an attitude of learning — an openness and even an exaltation that marks real education? Describe how your early experience of the divine through nature has focused and altered your existence. How has your early relationship with the "primary sacrament" contributed to your unfolding?

Drawing, painting, sculpting (even finger painting and sculpting in the mud), weaving and other art forms similarly engage the imagination and create the optimal environment for learning at a deep level. Reflect on the creative flow and the quality of absorption in your early, or recent, attempts at art. Was there a quality of inspiration similar to your connection to the natural world?

Inside each raindrop
swims the sun.
Inside each flower
breathes the moon.
Inside me dwell
two million stars
One for each of my
ancestors.

—Nancy Wood

Teaching and learning revolve around understanding the world, the objects, creation, beauty, scientific precision and common sense.

—Paulo Freire

The soul should always stand ajar, ready to welcome the ecstatic experience.

—Emily Dickinson

Planet Home

Pondering

We all desire to find our home and be at home. Streets bulge with the homeless — adults, children, animals. In a sense, every species is in search of a home; the pursuit and passion for ecology is the desire to find a home on Earth. On one very important level the bioregion of our childhood may truly be home for us.

> The world is the arena for the historical realization of the kingdom of God.
>
> —Leonardo Boff

In the same way, in a time when Earth is endangered by mistreatment, we can look to indigenous people for wisdom and guidance. The Dene people of Canada's Northwest Territories, for example, refer to the Earth as their flesh, their blood, their life. Their relationship to the land of their birth fashions their self-awareness, wisdom and sense of unity for all life.

For me, the St. Clair River in Ontario is home. The last time I drove there, my spirits lifted perceptibly as I approached the river. My heart told me that I was *home.*

The ecological movement has made us sensitive to our damaged planet. In many of us it arouses a passion to defend, protect and reverence our homes. We want to do everything we can to revise society's ideology of "more is better."

> We must widen our circle of compassion. We must embrace all living creation. We must affirm the whole of nature in its beauty.
>
> —McGregor Smith, Jr.

Our call today is to find "a spirituality of place." We embrace our home as sacred and as a manifestation of the divine.

Soulwork

In order to transform our culture in this time of transition, we need to reflect critically on our personal and societal experience. When we gather in groups to reflect on our collective experience, we can integrate the past and focus on the future. We can also keep a journal, share dreams and participate in base groups as ways to deepen our connection to the Earth as home and to focus our actions for the Earth.

Today, return your attention to the land and remember your ancestors; reflect on oneness with the Earth. Walk gently on the Earth.

Make every day an "Earth day," a day to pledge your energy to the awareness and practice of a sacred ecology in your purchases, your relationships and your life.

We humans cannot live in dignity and freedom while we exploit and pollute our planetary home.

—Diarmuid O'Murchu

Moments of the Unexpected

Pondering

It was Christmas morning. I was sitting with my sister in her car. As we headed toward St. Catherine's Church for Mass, I heard a voice from behind the wheel say: "This is your real Christmas present, Jim. I'm getting a new car in January, and I'm going to give this one to you. We'll have it shipped to you out west."

I thought for a moment about what I had just heard. My first response was, "Are you sure you know what you're doing?"

She assured me that, yes, she had thought about it for some time and that this was a firm and considered decision.

Later that day, as I was reading my favorite Christmas book, *Starlight,* by John Shea, I realized that what had happened on the way to church was indeed a reminder of the deeper meaning of Christmas. That meaning was truly more profound than the upgrading of a beat-up Buick to a late-model Camry. It was much more about the reality that the Incarnation was an unexpected surprise. Christmas is about a gift, about seeing the important events of life as moments that are unexpected.

> This is the fullness of time — when the Son of God is begotten in you . . . . in this birth you will discover all blessing.
>
> —Meister Eckhart

So often the pivotal events of our lives occur without warning or preparation. As I look back over my own years, it becomes increasingly clear to me that the events that have most profoundly shaped my life, often deeply altering my existence, have been unearned, unplanned and, occasionally, even for a time, unrecognized.

On this Christmas Day, jarred into awareness by my sister's generosity, I awoke to a renewed meaning of the Incarnation — the meaning of gift, grace and the infusion of goodness that Christmas invites us to remember and reflect upon.

Suddenly the stories of the three wise men and the bringing of the gifts at Epiphany took on new meaning. The Incarnation *continues* as we give and receive our gifts, as we manifest the divine effusion of newness in all aspects of our existence.

Christmas has many meanings. The birth of the sun (solstice) and the giving of gifts remind us of the ongoing event of the Incarnation manifest in the light of morning, the gesture of a loved one, the reception of an unexpected gift. In the words of John Shea, life is about waking up to welcome and celebrate our awareness of "the God who fell from heaven."

Soulwork

Today, or soon, set aside some time for yourself, at least twenty minutes. Put on some instrumental music that you enjoy.

In your mind or in your journal, make an inventory of gifts you have received that have altered your existence. (For example, perhaps the initial encounter with the person who is now your spouse or an event that altered your career path — an occurrence that brought you to the realization that your deeper destiny is not really in your hands.)

Focus your awareness on those day-to-day events that come to you as intuitions, inner promptings, sacred impulses — events that alter and illuminate your daily journey and often set the stage for more significant events that contribute to your life in mysterious and significant ways.

When you have completed your inventory, consider drawing a "map" of your life's journey. Celebrate those turning points that have been incarnational moments in your existence. Reflect on each of these turning points, even the ones that have appeared as crises — and savor their meaning and implications for your life.

The people are quite right in a way when they call this the "birthday of the Lord, the new sun." ... We gladly accept the name, because at the coming of the savior not only is humankind saved but the very light of the sun is renewed.

—G. K. Chesterton

I found a bottomless abyss at my feet and out of it came . . . arising I know not from where, the current which I dare to call my life.

—Teilhard de Chardin

Examining Our Feelings for the Natural World

Pondering

Imagine that you live on a farm and the only creatures you relate to are the cows. Not the fields, the corn, the chickens, the horses — only the cows. If this were the case, people would say you were out of balance, and they would be right. Today, people like Theodore Rozak, author of *The Voice of the Earth*, are reminding us that psychology is out of balance in a similar way. It is *anthropocentric*, which basically means "human centered."

Psychology teaches us to examine our feelings toward our parents, siblings, partner and friends. This is all very well, even essential. But we also need to understand how we feel and act toward the natural world. What is our emotional response to what Thomas Berry has named the "human's rage against the natural world"?

In the past our feelings and response to Earth have not been examined from the perspective of relationship, for we are just as much in relationship with nature as with our family, community and country. Today, as we become more ecologically aware, that is beginning to shift. We are realizing that we need to develop and explore our relationships with each member of the Earth community, not just our fellow humans. One of the great paradoxes of the human condition is the mystery of the incarnation; we are both divine and finite, sacred and limited. When we fail to honor our limitations, we tend to dominate and destroy, or we cave in and fail to fully actualize our gifts. It is our gift and our challenge to honor and examine the limits of our lives and celebrate the beauty of our planetary home.

> What is crucial for a viable future is a religious spirit that connects us to Earth.
>
> —Elizabeth Johnson

> Each day
> The Earth awaits
> The light of
> Your love
> And thanks you.

Soulwork

A significant part of the spiritual journey is about weaving together constellations of relationships that are harmonious and just. Bringing honesty, integrity and open communication to our relationships is a way to begin. Our spiritual journey is a response to what we most deeply believe about justice in relation to humans as well as the entire Earth community. After careful reflection about what you most deeply believe, reflect on the present direction of your spiritual journey. Then, you might want to write your personal "Canticle for the Earth." Post it where you will see it and reflect upon it often.

Canticle for the Earth

Where there are
   ruptures in creation,
We are called to bring
   peace.
Where there is
   disquietude,
We are invited to create
   balance.
Where there is discord,
   we are attuned to
   harmony.
In and through the pain
   of our planet
We are called to make
   our Easter with the
   Earth.
From collapse and
   devastation
We discover within the
   risen heart of the
   universe
      cosmic peace,
      profound harmony,
      deep balance,
      compassionate
      resonance
   and geo-justice
   for the Earth.

Justice and the Monks of Skid Row

Pondering

There was a time when I thought that justice-making was primarily a matter of keeping the rules. Being a keeper of the rules began to lose its appeal for me when I realized that rules are often made by the rich for the benefit of the rich. And then justice began to mean being on the side of the oppressed. As an associate pastor I found an affinity with the uprooted and other homeless people. During an urban plunge among the homeless in Toronto, I wrote the following reflection:

The Monks of Skid Row

A strange breed of monks, these 12,000 derelicts of life,
    these lovable genial isolated human beings.
They live with a past not to be forgotten,
    a present built out of isolation,
    and a future that promises and hopes for nothing.
These monks of the inner city are more alone
    than the strictest contemplative —
    and often more redeemed
    as they traffic in their currency of cigarettes,
    where to get beer, a bed, a meal, a job and sometimes money.
They are selfless and concerned,
    these islands of humanity boasting of a day's work
    and regretting a wasted life.
They trust NO ONE as they walk
    their silent world of pain and fear,
    this order of the street, people without futures, without rights.
Poor, pushed, passed by and possessed
    by those who provide beds and food,
    keeping them on one aimless treadmill of life.
They live without solutions,
    with no one listening to what they say,
    no one asking them to talk,

The day of my spiritual awakening was the day I saw — and knew I saw — all things in God and God in all things.

—Mechtild of Magdeburg

Practice justice, it will heal your soul.

—Jim Wallis

106

inviting them to spill, to drain
the poison from their lives —
a poison that festers in nightmares, alcohol,
fear of work, passive acceptance of mistreatment,
unexpressed anger and fear.

Soulwork

Plan and carry out a *direct* action for a poor or homeless person this week: Volunteer one day at a homeless shelter or other place where you will come into personal contact with one of the "least of these," the *anawim.*

It is all of a piece,
justice for the poor
people, justice for the
earth.

—Jane Blewett

Who is our neighbor:
The Samaritan? The
outcast? The enemy?
Yes, yes, of course, but
it is also the whale, the
dolphin and the rain
forest. Our neighbor is
the entire community
of life, the entire
universe. We must love
it all as our self.

—Brian Patrick

Energy for Justice-Making

Pondering

Energy for justice-making comes from many emotions and virtues — nobility, anger, desire, outrage, pain, aspiration, struggle and hope. I myself was drawn into the world of justice-making and community organizing for many reasons: among others, my own anger and feelings of being an outsider, and my vision and hope for a better world.

What I have learned about justice-work, and about myself, is that we both have a shadow side. Each of us has wounds, but we are called to participate despite our pain and our limitations — perhaps *from* the pain of our wounds. Justice-making is the way we discover who we are, the vehicle through which we contribute to the Earth and its people.

I had the privilege of attending a concert given by Harry Belafonte. He shared a conversation he had had with Nelson Mandela about setbacks in U.S. society. Mandela's response is a wonderful statement about the meaning of working for justice: "You'll just have to keep at it until they're all one."

Soulwork

How do you understand the relationship between justice and love? Would you agree that they are, in fact, the same?

Sharing food and remembering our roots reminds us of the Last Supper, a cosmic meal of liberation, a commemoration of service and compassion. The next time you gather with friends and family, take time to remember your ancestors. Celebrate family stories that underpin your desire for freedom and justice.

Energy for justice-making — action taken on behalf of justice and participation in the transformation of the world fully appears to us as a constitutive dimension of the preaching of the Gospel.

—1971 Synod of Bishops

There is a passionate groundswell of the imagination.

—Mark Dowie

Decide to be a global citizen
A good inhabitant of the planet Earth
A member of the great human family
Pray, think, act, feel, and love globally
And you will aggrandize yourself to the outer limits of being.

—Robert Muller

108

The Great Hunger

Pondering

In was early Sunday morning, and I was on my bike headed for the YMCA. As I passed the city post office, I saw four people in blankets and sleeping bags on the steps; they had not yet "got up to face another day." These homeless ones are profound reminders that in our society there is a deep hunger for home.

These four people brought to my mind the biblical story of the multiplication of the loaves and fishes, also a story of hunger and of great abundance. I thought of the thirty-three percent of the world's population that had gone to bed hungry the night before, about the thousands and thousands of children who would die of hunger today. I pondered the "loaves and fishes" and the homeless ones on the post office steps in Berkeley. I wondered how this can happen in a society where overeating fuels a multimillion-dollar weight-loss industry. I remembered the famines that have ravaged many lands throughout history, and the deep hunger that affected my own ancestors a century and a half ago when their crops failed in Ireland.

Later, as I showered and then prepared for the liturgy, the immense pathos of hunger and homelessness flooded my consciousness. I asked myself this question: Is the reason we as a people feel incapable of housing the homeless and feeding the hungry because we ourselves are starved — starved for an experience that can strengthen our souls and nourish our hearts? If we could satisfy our desire for the divine and feel at home in the universe, would we not then have the inner abundance to house and feed those in need and to celebrate with enthusiasm — with Spirit? I have a deep conviction that the answer is *yes*.

Soulwork

Spend some time today awakening to the profound pathos in our midst. The hungry and homeless continually remind us of the unhealed pain that ravages our cities and

The dream changes again
Like the cloud-swung wind
And he is not so sure now
If his mother was right
When she praised the man
Who made the field his
bride.

—Patrick Kavanaugh,
"The Great Hunger"

One eats in holiness and the table becomes an altar

—Martin Buber

I saw Christ today
At a street corner stand.
In the rags of a beggar
he stood.

—Patrick Kavanaugh

dulls the spirits of so many who are fortunate to be fed and clothed.

Then spend some time in prayer or meditation to get in touch with the place of abundance deep within. Satisfy your desire for the divine and experience being at home in the universe. Then, out of that place of abundance, take another look at the hungry and homeless. Journal about — or, better yet, act on — your observations.

> I am coming to realize that the famine experience has not ended . . . until the world's children are safe from famine today, until we live in a world where all of us are truly home.
>
> —Tom Hayden

> When a member of a family suffers and dies, the other members grieve. Since we know now that millions of men die of hunger every year, we can no longer live as before.
>
> Lord, it isn't easy to feed the world!
>
> —Michel Quoist

The City: Secular and Sacred

Pondering

Growing up near Detroit, I learned early in life what a city is. It is a place where machines are made — in this case the automobile; it is truly the Motor City. Cities are largely the result of the industrial revolution; they are places where people have lived in close proximity to one another in order to be near their work. The term *inner city* names the congestion around the factory and workplace. It is also a place where minorities live: black people from cotton fields of the South seeking work in the factories in the North; immigrants from Europe and later Asia, the Caribbean and Central America seeking freedom from political conflict and a better standard of living. City is the place of the poor and oppressed.

Harvey Cox's *The Secular City* (1963) along with Gibson Winter's *New Creation as Metropolis* (1965) drew attention to the fear, the alienation and the absence of the sacred in urban life.

As I reflect now on the meaning of Geo-Justice for the city, I realize that there is a profound connection between social and ecological justice, between the crack in the ozone layer and the crack sold on the street. Why are toxic dump sites inevitably placed in minority neighborhoods? Why do senior citizens' facilities get located near cemeteries? Why does nuclear testing take place on the lands of indigenous people? What is the connection between oppressed people and the oppressed Earth?

In my questioning I saw that the inner city, the ghetto, is also sacred, that the city is as much Earth as rocks, water and trees. In a postindustrial and now emerging ecological age, the city is both the result of devastation and a vehicle for new life. We must "green" our cities — and "green" our souls.

We still need the mediating structures of community organization in order to make our cities more viable and our hearts more verdant and open. An Earth ethic for the city will involve promoting life in our urban centers, especially

> The city has become the universal magnet, while rural life has lost its savor . . . . To restore a proper balance between city and rural life is perhaps the greatest task in front of modern man.
>
> —E. F. Schumacher

> The word
> is living,
> being,
> spirit,
> all verdant greening,
> all creativity.
>
> —Hildegard of Bingen

111

the life of the weakest. We need to end the violence against people and nature and work toward harmony and the full expression of life. We need to take up the challenge to partnership, to foster and protect the destiny and health of this planet in city life.

A new book needs to be written. I would call it *Sacred City: The New Jerusalem*. In such a city people will express passion and compassion for all expressions of life. It will be a place where dreams are fostered and a vision draws us into the future. When Martin Luther King, Jr., stood at the foot of the Washington Monument more than three decades ago, he spoke of a dream of racial justice. It is time to enunciate a vision of personal and planetary liberation through social and ecological justice.

The New Story has the capacity to energize our spirit, elevate our vision and foster a sense of hope. We need to fully and dynamically integrate it into the story of Geo-Justice so that justice-making as celebration can transcend the glum plodding that is so endemic in the lives of many cultural workers in our day.

Soulwork

Your approach to life, to your work, to justice-work, is in many ways a function of your story. Catherine Ingram's *In the Footsteps of Gandhi* makes important connections between story and social justice. Today is an opportunity to trace the connections between your journey and your commitment to compassion. How has your story shaped your connections to justice? How has your woundedness given you an energetic and compassionate heart?

I have a dream ....
—Martin Luther King, Jr.

Some men see things and say, "Why?" I see things that never were and say, "Why not?"
—Robert Kennedy

Presence and Perception

Pondering

The world in which we live reflects how we see reality. For example, Detroit and the automobile reflect a mechanistic worldview. But the industrial revolution and its commitment to create a world of wonder and possession that "Motor City" symbolizes is crumbling, while decay and devastation have begun to accelerate. Poverty, unemployment and oppression are proliferating across the planet, especially in the large urban sprawls that dot the world. We are being challenged to live differently.

> The philosophers have only interpreted the world. The thing, however, is to change it.
>
> —Karl Marx

What are some of the changes we are being called to make? In our spirituality, we are being challenged to see that the Divine is not just spirit. The Incarnation reminds us that God is both matter and spirit, that all dimensions of life are sacred. With this in mind, we are challenged to use technology to enhance life on the Earth, not to add to the destruction.

Enhancing our human presence and transforming the culture involve finding forms that allow us to express our deepest fascination, passions and dreams, art and language, as vehicles of right livelihood. Indeed, children grow away from their families and homes in order to develop their unique personalities and gifts, only to return as adults to come to terms with their ancestral roots and their traditions; in the same way, the human community, having abandoned the Earth during the industrial era, is now beginning to return.

> Farmers sustain the land to be handed down to their children, corporations are uninterested in the next generation.
>
> —Rosemary Radford Ruether

This return involves moving from independence to *inter*dependence, from distance to more integral and mutually enhancing relationships. More and more we are moving toward becoming participants in the community of life, more and more infused with consciousness and common sense.

Soulwork

Acknowledging the gifts and achievements of others is a powerful, compassionate and irreplaceable part of growth and a key gesture in coming to genuine interconnectedness.

From this perspective we are able to amplify another's gifts while preserving our own integrity. We are able to dissolve the illusion of separateness that permeates our culture to our mutual disadvantage.

Today, make a point of finding something to affirm or praise in a family member, a friend, social acquaintance or colleague. Do the same tomorrow . . . and the next day . . . and the next . . . .

We need to reenter the forest and remember the lessons learned on the pathway to the moon.
—Loren Eiseley

Functional Relationships

Pondering

For most of my life, I have deeply resisted and distrusted bureaucracy and the power exercised by authority. I think my interest in community organizing came from the desire or impulse to resist the power structure, to be "true to my Irish heritage" and perhaps to stand "against the government."

But as the years have gone by, I have finally realized that it is not possible to have it always my own way. It seems to be a necessity of life to have a "spirituality of bureaucracy." The question is: How do we deal with relationships that are dysfunctional and oppressive?

On one level it is important not to be overcome or obsessed with those who oppose us. We must let them be; they have their own lives, as we do. When we withdraw our resistance and free ourselves from our emotional obsession with them, we are free to be more fully ourselves and to act more effectively for our own purposes.

Recently much has been written about "dysfunctional relationships" and their connection to families, communities or individuals. This is simply another language for being "too attached," for being "off-center." It's having our emotional balance so tilted in the direction of the other that we lose track of ourselves and of our own inner wisdom and balance — and of our capacity for functional relationships with others, creation and God.

As we stand at the precipice, we are invited to understand deeply the connection between internalized oppression and the injustice that is so prevalent in our country and world.

With new energy and perspective, we take off the blinders of narrowness and fear and move forward with energy, confidence and courage.

It is when we confront our reluctance and take up the challenge before us that we will truly take on the role of the prophet and find the inner strength to go forward. In this

To change one's life:
- ♦ Start immediately
- ♦ Do it flamboyantly
- ♦ No exceptions
  (no excuses)

—William James

The country is hungry for spiritual politics.

—Jim Wallis

115

new moment of grace we will discover the courage to push through to a future of newness and justice — a planetary Pentecost.

Soulwork

A woman walking along the beach in Hawaii noticed an enormous number of starfish on the shore. All these starfish would die when the tide went out. A man walking by saw the woman picking up a starfish and returning it to the sea. He said, "Don't you realize that there is nothing you can do that will make a difference? These starfish are going to die." She simply looked at him and smiled. Then she said, "It's going to make a difference to *this* one."

Remind yourself each day that you *do* make a difference in the seemingly small things you do in your life.

It is our belief in roses that brings them into bloom.

—French proverb

Whatsoever you do may seem insignificant, but it is most important that you do it.

—Gandhi

116

The Structural Dance

Pondering

Institutional life presents many challenges; we all have our own level of tolerance for structure. Some of us are institutional prophets who can toil within the bowels of organization. Others hold a more anarchical stance. They feel the need for freedom from structures in their lives to be fully who they are. The work of Dorothy Day, co-founder of the Catholic Worker, is typical of the latter approach.

No matter where we are on the spectrum, some participation in structures is part of all our lives. The trick is always to maximize participation *and* enhance the contribution of each person's gift to the larger effort. But the process is not always evident or the procedure clear.

Sometimes people on the edges focus on a personal agenda. Others, who are more centrally located and whose personal needs are already met and protected, may find themselves more concerned about the larger picture.

Whatever our choices and the results of these choices, dealing with structure, self-interest, participation and the sharing of our gifts remain components of our path. How we deal with these issues is important in our spiritual journey; the answers will continue to shape and focus our future, and self-knowledge and courage will shape our responses.

> Individual justice is connected to international issues.
>
> —Megan McKenna

> We all must seek a paradigm that will enable Gaia to live and all beings in creation, especially human beings, to exist in solidarity.
>
> —Leonardo Boff

Soulwork

Take a long rope and make a circle on the floor (or in your mind). At the center, place a placard that says POWER. At some point on the circumference place a placard that reads FREEDOM. Move freely within the circle. Stand at the center and reflect on your feelings. After a time, move to the edge and reflect on your responses. Then take some time to record your feelings in your journal; in particular, be aware of what your body revealed to you in this exercise.

Take an inventory of the institutions in your life: How does each meet your need? What changes would you propose regarding church, politics, school, your employer?

> Power, like a desolating
>   pestilence,
> Pollutes whate'er it
>   touches; and
>   obedience,
> Bane of all genius,
>   virtue, freedom, truth,
> Makes slaves of men,
>   and of the human frame
> A mechanized
>   automaton.
>
> —Percy Bysshe Shelley

Ritual

Pondering

All the great activities of life are symbolic.

—Daniel Berrigan

Life is sometimes difficult and demanding. It is easy to become caught up in the work world, to live "on the surface" in response to the demands of daily existence. Yet, unknowingly or knowingly, there is a hunger in our life; some part of us yearns to reach into our depths. It is out of this hunger that we need to create, participate in and foster ritual.

Rituals can be simple acts that express our memories and experiences. Our family rituals center around particular events or holidays: how we celebrate Christmas or Thanksgiving, how we respond to tragedy, how we rejoice in new life, how we mark the milestones of life.

Rituals take us beyond words into mystery; they are about meaning, destiny and depth. The liturgy is a ritual that recalls and enacts the basic beliefs of our tradition. Rituals are sacramental because they bring about what they signify. For example, the Eucharist not only symbolizes the unity of eating a common meal together; it also brings that unity about. We become companions in the breaking of the bread.

Rituals are a central part of life . . . . They connect us with our past, define our present life and show us a path to our future.

—Evan Imber-Black and Janine Roberts
Rituals for Our Times

Rituals are the human way of bringing greater meaning and more profound expression to our lives. I remember the French Canadian food that my mother would prepare for Christmas. I remember my father planting potatoes on Good Friday, being true to his Irish roots. I remember gathering apples in the fall. Each of these rituals, and many others, held a meaning beyond their mere expression. They were powerful and satisfying; rituals reach to our heart and soul through silence, symbol, process, proclamation, movement and sound.

Pass on the whole story.
—Alla Rene Bozarth

Soulwork

Take a few moments to think about the rituals in your life. How did you celebrate holidays as a child? Which of those traditions do you still practice? Have you developed new traditions in your adult life? How did they come about?

118

What traditions will you hand down to your children or others?

Reflect on your feelings about the traditions of your past. Get in touch with the sense-memories they invoke — the sounds, smells, tastes, appearances and textures that help form part of your very being.

What rituals have marked the major transitions in your life, the rites of passage, the movement through a crisis to a new level of maturity? What rituals might help mark the cultural transition from the precipice toward a new millennium?

Finally, consider the role of Earth in your rituals. Did you go for sleigh rides? Swim in the moonlight? Roast marshmallows at a bonfire in the woods? How do you feel about Earth right now?

Teach your children what we have taught our children — that the earth is our mother . . . . Whatever befalls the earth befalls the sons and daughters of the earth. We did not weave the web of life; we are merely a strand in it. Whatever we do to the web, we do to ourselves.

—Chief Seattle

Rites of passage assist the recognition of the passage . . . invite exploration to confront the developmental tasks at this time . . . (then) the third aspect of the rites of passage comes into view — celebration of the transition into a new stage of life.

—Evelyn and James Whitehead

Transition

Pondering

Change sometimes involves deep and profound shifts in our way of being; like turbulent water, such transitions are sometimes precarious, yet always buoyant and consistently fertile with the promise of new birth. To navigate the waters of transition successfully requires that we access the wisdom of the past, prepare for the challenges of the future and respond fully and creatively to the present moment of grace.

An important vehicle for initiating change and responding to its challenge is the network. An interconnected web, a network is a vehicle for relationship rather than a structure for the delivery of a service. A network provides a context for spontaneity in an unpredictable world sometimes best described as a three-dimensional pool game.

During times of transition, people come together and discover their allies, identify their strengths and explore the potential for growth. They can listen to one another, learn from each other's inner wisdom and look toward the future with hope.

Successfully navigating through a major transition requires a tolerance for turbulence and uncertainty. We trust that balance and direction will emerge from what appears to be a sea of chaos. In working through transition we need to remember, and to be immersed in, our connection with the Divine, the infinite source of resources to meet our present predicament. The words of Dag Hammerskjold come to mind:

> For all that has been, thanks;
> for all that will be, yes.

> [We need] a richly celebrated life, connected to society and nature, woven into the culture of family, nation and globe.
>
> —Thomas Moore

> When I dare to be powerful, to use my strength in the service of my vision, then it becomes less and less important whether I am afraid.
>
> —Audre Lourde

Soulwork

A process in times of transition:

♦ List in your journal the options that are available to you in dealing with the upcoming changes in your life;

♦ Inventory your gifts and competencies as you analyze which of the options you are best able to fulfill;

120

- ◆ Create time and space for prayerful meditation to open to a revelatory moment, a moment of grace and insight;
- ◆ Consult trusted colleagues and friends;
- ◆ Make a choice, and then invest yourself fully in the implications of that choice;
- ◆ Continue to be open to the knowledge and insights that are revealed to you as you live out the choice you made.

Not in his goals but in his transitions
man is great.

—Ralph Waldo Emerson

The only wrong thing, perhaps, is permanently hesitating on the verge of courage.

—Sue Monk Kidd

Gatherings:
A Clarion Call of Hope

Pondering

In the spring we met in Boston; the "first gathering" for Brothers of Earth. A wonderful variety of men came: computer programmers and educational administrators, pastors and counselors, teachers and students, retreat directors and businessmen, friends and new acquaintances, and more — from California to Maine, Ontario to North Carolina, Texas to Prince Edward Island. We came to receive information and reflect on our common commitment to Earth.

In the fall I was in Washington, D.C., responding to a letter from Anthony Padovano of CORPUS. We came to join with people from around the country to respond to the question, "How can people involved in social justice, church reform and spirituality work together to amplify our efforts and achieve our common goals?"

> At the center of the human heart is a longing for an absolute good, a longing which is always there and is never appeased by any object in this world.
>
> —Simone Weil

As we pondered the question, we felt energized and inspired by the commitment and accomplishments of others in the room. Once again, people came from centers and projects whose long-term efforts have impacted the landscape of justice, church and spirituality across North America. Among those represented were Call to Action, Center for Action and Contemplation, Quixote Center, Center for Concern, Sophia Center, Network, Future Church, and more.

As in Boston, people came to Washington with imagination and dreams, honesty and directness, pain and possibility, with a desire to listen and a need to be heard, with an intuition toward reciprocity and a strategy toward building a coalition. We came together convinced that "we can do together what we can never do alone." We came to form a coalition of hope, to feel the fire of the moment and the possibility of tomorrow.

> We can do together what we can never do alone.
>
> —Paulo Freire

We came together busy and challenged in our present work yet somehow convinced that collaboration and common effort are a critical basis for what awaits us in the twenty-first century.

We came together, savoring our victories as well as feeling the pain of resistance and sometimes defeat. We came because the invitation touched our hearts, and we left knowing that we were not alone in the struggle. We left energized with a fresh hope for the children and a bridge for us all into the twenty-first century.

Soulwork

- ◆ Reflect on the people you feel connected to — in your family, community, parish and workplace.
- ◆ Consider calling some people together to share your stories and dreams.
- ◆ What gatherings are taking place in your area that you might consider participating in?
- ◆ Make a list of people who inspire you, whether you know them or simply know about them. Think of ways to join energies with them to participate in a "coalition of hope."

Gatherings of Hope

Impulses toward belonging
Evoke the possibility of hope
As each heart hears an invitation
And begin to coalesce.

Wonderful tomorrows
Beckon from this precipice
    of new beginnings
Where we gather to transcend
    our current call
As we bridge together our
Collective actions filled with hope.

Once again the challenge is announced
As we "arise and go"
To that yet-unnamed precipice place
And there respond to the
Clarion call for hope.

> We have all known the long loneliness and we have learned that the only salvation is love and that love comes with community.
>
> —Dorothy Day

> Tell me, what is it you plan to do
> With your one wild and precious life?
>
> —Mary Oliver

123

To Begin Again

Pondering

What we call the beginning is often the end. And to make an end Is to make a beginning The end is where we start from.

—T.S. Eliot

Newspapers announce the "year in review." Television offers pictorial portraits of the last 365 days. We recall those who have died in the past year and celebrate those newly born since last January 1. Millions around the country watch those crowded into Times Square in New York celebrate the countdown to the New Year. And more and more cities provide "First Night" celebrations, ushering in the New Year with performing artists in a safe and peaceful place for families, friends and neighbors.

All of these moments that mark the end of one year and the beginning of another are invitations to the human spirit to move into the future with the hope that tomorrow can be better than today. Hope for a better future burns fervently in the human heart.

I don't measure America by its achievements but by its potential.

—Shirley Chisholm

The cultural events of a First Night celebration, such as the ones I recently attended in Akron, Ohio, and in Manasquan, New Jersey — with their Broadway, bluegrass and traditional Irish music — not only point toward the next year but herald a promise of renewed energy and hope for tomorrow. That hope holds a possibility of the experience of community that includes every species of the Earth. It points to a renewed determination to create together the conditions necessary to usher in the new era that awaits us as we look back and dare to move forward and begin yet again.

Soulwork

It's not over. It will never be over Until we begin to speak the words Of movement again.

—Jim Wallis

The call of Geo-Justice is to fashion the seamless garment between social and ecological justice; the culmination of the task is to arrive at a new creation, the context of the reign of God, where peace and community will take root and be celebrated — the fulfillment of the *kingdom*.

List the events, ideas or visions of the future that invigorate your spirit and fill your life with promise, replacing the burden of existence with enthusiasm, courage

124

and a renewed spirit. Reflect on the items on your list. Allow yourself to savor the hope and sense of recommitment that flow from your reflection. Think about the following questions:

♦ How do you envision personal, communal and global relationships that are healthy and that promote peace and justice? How do you visualize the new community of life on Earth?
♦ What is needed to support such a sacred and integral ecology?
♦ How can you contribute to the coming of such an ecological age, the coming of the *kingdom*, a planetary Pentecost?
♦ What is your fondest hope for the new millennium?

It is now only dawn.

—Pope John XXIII

Angels, as this year
    now nears its end
Fold their wings, as
    gently down they bend,
Rent and broken hopes
    on earth to mend.
May they find us ready
    to rise!
Angels, at the dawn of a
    new year
Spread bright wings and
    rise, and rise from here
Raising us to Heights
    we crave, yet fear.
May they find us
    daring!

—Br. David
Steindl-Rast, OSB

V.

Epilogue

Good news.
But if you ask me what it is, I know not.
It is a track of feet in the snow.
It is a lantern showing a path.
It is a door set open.

—G. K. Chesterton

When hope crumbles, everything crumbles.
Hope is the oxygen of our souls.

—Hendryk Skolimowski

Theology is always exploratory and never final.

—Tissa Balasuriya

The part of you called "Sophia" is so alive in all creation.
The trees, the animals, the earth, the sky
and all that is in between,
I am surrounded with goodness that nourishes me with new life.

—Helen Wilke

The past has revealed to me the structure of the future.

—Teilhard de Chardin

Hope is the memory of the future.

—Gabriel Marcel

I will make all things well and you will see yourself
that every kind of thing will be well.

—Julian of Norwich

Epilogue:
Entering the New Millennium
The Journey of a Soul in a Time of Transition

Move from within.
Don't move the way
Fear wants you to.
—Rumi

Forget the incident.
Remember the lesson.
—Zina Jacques

In many ways our personal transitions are microcosms of the larger shift that is taking place within the planet and humanity as we prepare for and participate in the great work of the twenty-first century.

The catalyst for the following reflection, an Eastertime catharsis titled "From Turbulance to Transformation," was an event that changed the course of my life in a way that I found very unsettling. Suddenly everything that I believed was called into question. I wasn't sure that what I had achieved in the past had any value — unsure about what I was called to in the future. The present was chaos; my life lacked order and direction.

Like you, I have felt the pain of uncertainty and disappointment and the outrage of being misunderstood. The fear and feeling that something was ending — on a deep level it felt like life itself was being taken away, without gratitude, appreciation or the possibility of things being different.

As a child, I was separated from my mother because of her illness. At that time I felt that my life was in danger, that I was being separated from the source of life itself. Now, as an adult, I have felt echoes of that early separation: when a relationship ended, when my health was endangered and when my livelihood was uncertain.

127

I asked myself then, and I ask myself now: What do I do in the face of personal threat or loss? How do we creatively respond to a lack of gratitude for our efforts, to a feeling of unexpected violation or betrayal, to character and "soul" assassination? And how do we expose our wounds without imposing blame? My answers to these questions remain without full clarity or confidence.

One lesson I have learned is that the events of life and behavior of others are beyond my control. I am not in charge. My response to the events of personal or communal injustice that cause me pain is that I must make every effort to transform whatever patterns of oppression I recognize. I strive to respond with all the strength, wisdom and insight I can muster. Initially I give myself permission to express outrage at the injustices that come my way. Simultaneously, in the deepest way possible, I let go of how these events invaded my life. I acknowledge my pain and yet remain grounded in my trust that out of the turbulence of the chaos will emerge clarity and direction — that "in the larger arc of things" justice will reign. Saul Alinsky wrote, "The action is in the reaction." The wisdom of this statement reveals that when faced with unpredictable events that frighten and unsettle, it is important to stay grounded and not react. Our primary spiritual practice becomes one of staying in touch with our deepest self, receiving the support of friends, family and nature, and acknowledging our immersion in the divine embrace that reminds us of love, trust and the possibility of a better tomorrow.

From here on the precipice, we leave behind the past and take up the challenge to move forward and begin again. We recover from the shattering of plans and perceptions to experience more deeply than ever before the fire of our lives that will ignite the new possibilities that await us here on the precipice of a new era. Perhaps the new millennium will be truly a moment of grace and the twenty-first century a revelatory event in all our lives. As we are reminded today of the planetary crisis that confronts us, we emerge with a renewed sense of the sacred as we move forward from the precipice and engage in the soulwork that can make the new millennium the place of a planetary Pentecost.

From Turbulence to Transformation

The journey of a soul in a time of transition can feel like a ride down a turbulent river. The rapids of crisis and change are often precarious. In the upheaval the soul is sometimes submerged, gasping for air, swirling out of control. Yet when we can let go and trust the deepest current of life, we find that even in the most chaotic waters of change there is always a buoyancy, and the water is ever fertile with the promise of birth. Personal crises ever hold the possibility of passage to a new level of maturity, to a deeper, more compassionate ground of living. Successfully navigating these turbulent waters of transition requires accessing the wisdom of the past and preparing to meet the challenges of the future, while responding fully and creatively to the present moment of grace held within the crisis.

What is true of personal times of transition is also true in social and communal crises. Within each turbulent eddy of crisis there is a stillpoint of grace, a point for pondering the divine presence and gathering our resources to stay afloat. In this stillpoint we realize that we are not alone as we ride the rapids of change and transition. We realize that we can form networks that are vehicles for relationship as well as interconnecting webs that keep us afloat.

We come together to discover our allies, identify our strengths, explore our potential for growth, review our vision and develop strategies for coping with the changes taking place. We realize we are not just being taken for a ride, but can actually affect the course of our journey. When we come together and are provided with information and support, we listen to one another's voices, reflect on our inner promptings and adjust our course. This process enables us to look toward the future with hope — a future that will be realized from within the ever-expanding constellation of relationships and support.

In the stillpoint we become aware not only of our mutual support but of the Spirit that sustains us and provides us a vision of the possible to impel us on our journey. In this divine buoyancy we realize that accomplishing the work of transition requires tolerance for turbulence and uncertainty. This important capacity is accompanied by a radical trust that balance and direction will come out of what appears to be chaos. From this place of ambiguity and emerging order we continue Christ's work of shaping a shared destiny of planetary liberation and profound fulfillment, a process referred to as the coming of God's reign. For this work of transition only can be accomplished when it is nourished by an intimate experience of the Divine. Only when our individual and corporate efforts are grounded in God can we summon the necessary courage and strength to achieve what often appears overwhelming and impossible — the great work of realizing the historical mission of humanity as we welcome and usher in the age of justice, peace and the integrity of creation.

This new world view and the strategies and tactics that accompany its application are born out of the collective imaginations of scientists, artists, theologians and activists. When they — and all of us together — listen and respond to divine revelation as it is expressed in traditional ways as well as throughout creation and within the human spirit, these new understandings will extend into the area of cultural transformation. As we listen to the voiceless of the Earth, we take up the enormous challenges of restructuring education, religion and public and corporate life with the goal of ushering Earth and all its peoples into an era of harmony and peace. This fresh and anticipated moment promises to be personally enriching and beneficial for all creation.

To function in this new era will require decisive and collaborative action; the magnitude of the task will require a community of creative and dedicated people whose diverse backgrounds and gifts will be brought into focus by a transcendent and common goal.

As we engage in change, we realize that each moment of transition evokes memories of gratitude for what has gone before, for all we have received. Simultaneously, the waters of transition invite us to embrace the future. During this daring and delicate time of moving into an unknown future, the process of those engaged in this great adventure will be spirited, participatory and hopeful. A focus on the future will empower us to withstand the predictable tidal waves of resistance in the forms of accusation, innuendo and half-truths. Such turbulence ever calls us to return to the stillpoint of grace wherein we engage in the quest for the divine and the struggle to transcend ego-involvement and self-delusion. It is here in the fertile womb of silence that new vision is born, that we will discover our place and path in the larger drama of life.

The entire process of the soul in a time of such transition is focused and stabilized through connecting with trusted colleagues and doing everything possible to capture each precious moment as an opportunity to ignite a new consciousness, a new ethos and a new culture.

At all times on the immense journey toward a new understanding of the drama of our origins and destiny we will be energized by gratitude and freed by a capacity to surrender any impulse to dominate or control. Only then will the divine plan reveal itself in mysterious and powerful ways; only then will those engaged in the journey of transition be able to access the capacity to endure this profound period of growth, decline and renewal; only then will we be energized to move into the future from a context of radical reciprocity based on an affirmation of core values and commitments previously made.

Involvement in this prophetic effort will stretch the envelope of our imagination regarding what is possible and will thrust us into a future where there is full congruence between authority and self-initiative, vision and practice, lifestyle and engaged spirituality, personal integrity and professional responsibility. Always there will be an allegiance to a well-developed strategy to invent and execute programs in which leadership demonstrates a healthy disregard for status or stature. To accomplish this task each person must place performance over ego, continuity over chaos, trust over suspicion, gratitude over greed. Only in this way will it be possible to design and develop the delicate and prophetic vehicle so necessary and needed to usher in a new era. The values and vehicles necessary for the task have never been more needed.

As participants in this great transformation, we cannot stand outside the deep changes we aspire to and work toward. The unfolding future will invite new avenues of promise and participation, of commitment and collegiality. As we companion each other into the new era of consciousness and culture, we look back with praise and move forward with hope that the future will be better than all the past. In this new ethos and era, charity will be fostered, toxic triangulation[6] eliminated and the struggle for life affirmed on many levels.

The emerging goal of our journey will become ever more constant and clear — to liberate ourselves and all involved from personal oppression and the structures of domination. Inspired by a glimpse of newfound freedom and aroused by the struggle for fulfillment on a personal and cultural level, each of us will embrace this new moment of grace with rigorous effort and an engaged spiritual practice.

Strengthened by mental discipline and a willingness to embrace the magnitude of the task, convinced that each of us and our collective efforts are indeed "bathed in God," we move forward fully prepared to exercise the courage to create a vital constellation of functional relationships; from here each one will take up the challenge that is based on truth, conscious of the past and predicated on the vision of an enchanting future.

Sacred Earth

With gratitude and grace
we celebrate the story
of creation, liberation and us.
In blessing and brokenness
we restore hunger for newness
boiling from the wellsprings of our souls.
Here within wonder and surprise
we rediscover hope
and recognize once more the signature of God.

131

Notes

1. This, and all the following uncited margin quotes, are by Jim Conlon.

2. See Boniface Hanley, O.F.M., *Ten Christians* (Notre Dame, Ind.: Ave Maria Press, 1979).

3. The outline above finds its origin in the writing and work of Dr. Dorothy Donnelly, who teaches and writes in the San Francisco Bay area.

4. Stanley Krippner and David Feinstein, *Personal Mythology: The Psychology of Your Evolving Self* (Los Angeles: Jeremy Tarcher, 1988).

5. Rachel Carson, *The Silent Spring* (New York: Houghton Mifflin, 1962).

6. The term *toxic triangulation* refers to the pathological impact that happens when people do not communicate directly but rather through a third party.

VI.

Projects for an Ecological Age

Far beyond the halls of power and outside the media spotlight, these extraordinary, ordinary citizens are moving ahead with optimism and commitment to put in place the foundations of the new era in an atmosphere of experimentation, creativity, compassion, love and passion for life.

—David Korten

I recommend the following as approaches to preparing for and entering into the twenty-first century:

Meditation: Spend some twenty minutes each day in silence and solitude. Choose a location where you are in the presence of and enveloped by the natural world. Be present. Pay attention to and enter into communication with the presence of the divine in creation.

Revelatory moments: Conscious that the universe is the first revelation — the primary "book" about God) — spend time increasing your awareness of how the divine communes through the events of your existence. Reflect on these epiphanies of your life. Through dialogue and discernment work to achieve an increased understanding of their meaning for your life.

Reading: Through your interests, intuition and curiosity choose reading material that will sharpen your intellect, deepen your instincts and nourish your soul. Often in times of anxiety, worry, preoccupation or need, good reading can be healing and energizing. Follow your impulses and the recommendations of others in your pursuit of appropriate material. (The recommended reading section of this book lists many thought-provoking and spirit-expanding works.)

Silence: In your search of the universe, yourself and the divine, you can never have enough opportunities for silence. In today's dysfunctional culture of addictions and distractions, silence can connect you to the wellspring of your life, enrich your journey and foster the possibility of an inward space from which your intuition and self-knowledge emerge.

Prayer: The capacity to pay attention to and open yourself to the crises

133

and opportunities of the present time is an act of prayer; it is here that you are seized by mystery, gain the capacity to transcend self and embrace life in a new and renewed way.

Story: In telling the universe's story, reflecting on the stories of Scripture, recounting your country's story, exploring the cultural turning points of your life and examining your own narrative as a chapter in all of these larger stories, you find a radical, essential wisdom. This practice is irreplaceable if you are to be able to grow your soul here on the cusp of the twenty-first century.

Shared dream experience: Sharing your dreams of your place in the universe — of your role in bringing about he great transition into an ecological age — may be an essential practice as you enter the new millennium. Through your dreams you will achieve a clearer understanding of your role in the great work.

Friendship: Live with and learn from peoples of many cultures and traditions as creation embraces its hopeful and common journey into the twenty-first century.

Awareness of the anawim: Be aware of the issues of the poor of the world and in your community. Cultivate a lifestyle that promotes justice and peace.

A preferential option for the poor Earth: Practice an all-inclusive lifestyle and spirituality that supports the liberation and fulfillment of the entire Earth community.

A global perspective: Through your spirituality and life practices encourage an awareness of how the global economic system is dependent on addiction and how facing into this addiction would change humanity's relationship to the Earth. Adopt a lifestyle that promotes global economic sustainability and ecological security and understands work and ecological security as compatible.

A bioregional lifestyle: Practice paying attention to your local community of life. Spend time paying attention to what is going on in your region with regard to cultures, species and exploitation.

Base groups for Earth: Form, or join, a base group that gathers to support its participants in developing an understanding of the lifestyles and spirituality that are appropriate for and attuned to an intimate relationship with the natural world in your region.

Live biodynamically: Plant a garden. Research how to maintain your garden without using chemicals. Buy local produce in neighborhood stores. Support local farmers. Sponsor and participate in cooking classes using natural foods.

The following projects have emerged as cultural forms whose primary purpose is to animate the great transition into an ecological age. You may find them helpful on your journey:

Brothers of the Earth (cosponsored by
    Spirit Earth and Sophia Center)
Sophia Center
Holy Names College
3500 Mountain Blvd.
Oakland, CA 94619
Jim Conlon / John Surette

The Center for Reflection
    on the Second Law
8420 Camelia Drive
Raleigh, NC 27613

Center for the Story
    of the Universe
311 Rydell Avenue
Mill Valley, CA 94941
Brian Swimme / Bruce Bochte

The Connector
265 Grandview Drive
Kalispell, MT 59901
Milt Carlson

EarthLight
111 Fairmont Avenue
Oakland, CA 94611
Kurt Lauren deBoer

The Ecozoic Society
1405 Oakland Avenue
Durham, NC 27705
Herman Green

Environmental Ethics Institute
Miami Dade Community College
11011 SW 104th Street
Miami, FL 33176
McGregor Smith

Foundation for Global Community
222 High Street
Palo Alto, CA 94301
Karen Harwell / Wileta Birch

Genesis Farm —
    Earth Literacy Learning Center
Biodynamic Farming
41A Silver Lake Road
Blairstown, NJ 07825
Miriam MacGillis / Maureen Wild

Global Education Associates
475 Riverside Drive, Suite 1848
New York, NY 10115
Patricia Mische

Narrow Ridge Earth Literacy Center
Route 2, Box 125
Washburn, TN 37888
Bill Nickle

Shantivanam — The Forest Letter
22019 Meagher Road
Easton, KS 66020
Joe Nassal

Sisters of Earth / Earth Literacy Program
St. Mary's-of-the-Woods College
St. Mary of the Woods, IN 47876
Mary Lou Dolan

Sophia Center — Wisdom School
    Celebrating Earth, Art & Spirit
(Fully accredited graduate program)
Holy Names College
3500 Mountain Blvd.
Oakland, CA 94610
Jim Conlon

Spirit Earth:
    Spirituality for the Ecological Age
PO Box 318
Newton Centre, MA 02159
John Surette

The Transformative Learning Center
Ontario Institute for Studies in Education
University of Toronto
252 Bloor Street West
Toronto, Ontario, Canada M5S-1V6
Edmund O'Sullivan

VII.

Recommended Reading

ABRAMS, JEREMIAH, ed. *The Shadow in America: Reclaiming the Soul of a Nation*. Novato, Calif.: Natari Publishing, 1994.

ADAMS, CASS, ed. *The Soul Unearther*. New York: Jeremy Tarcher/Putnam Books, 1996.

ALINSKY, SAUL. *Reveille for Radicals*. New York: Vintage Books, 1969.

ALINSKY, SAUL. *Rules for Radicals*. New York: Random House, 1971.

ALLEN, PAUL, AND JOAN DERIS ALLEN. *Francis of Assisi's Canticle of the Creatures*. New York: Continuum, 1995.

BALASURIYA, TISSA. *Mary and Human Liberation*. Harrisburg, Penn.: Trinity Press International, 1997.

BARBOUR, IAN. *Religion and Science* (revised edition). Mahwah, N.J.: Paulist Press, 1997.

BATSTONE, DAVID, ed. *New Visions for the Americas: Religious Engagement and Social Transformation*. Minneapolis: Fortress Press, 1993.

BAUM, GREGORY. *Man Becoming — God in Secular Experience*. Garden City, N.Y.: Herder & Herder, 1971.

BELLAH, ROBERT, et al. *The Good Society*. New York: Alfred Knopf, 1991.

BERRY, JAMES. "Circular 191." Raleigh, N.C.: The Center for Reflection on the Second Law, May 1991.

BERRY, THOMAS AND BRIAN SWIMME. *The Universe Story*. San Francisco: Harpers, 1992.

BERRY, THOMAS. "The Ecozoic Era." E. F. Schumacher Society Lectures. October 1991.

BERRY, THOMAS. *Riverdale Papers*. Unpublished manuscript.

BERRY, THOMAS. *The Dream of the Earth*. San Francisco: Sierra Club Books, 1988.

BOFF, LEONARDO. *Cry of the Earth, Cry of the Poor*. Maryknoll, N.Y.: Orbis Books, 1995.

BOFF, LEONARDO. *Ecology and Liberation — A New Paradigm*. Maryknoll, N.Y.: Orbis Books, 1995.

BUTALA, SHARON. *The Perfection of the Morning: An Apprenticeship in Nature*. Toronto: HarperCollins, 1994.

CAPRA, FRITJOF. *The Web of Life*. New York: Anchor Books, 1996.

CHAPPLE, CHRISTOPHER, ed. *Ecological Prospects*. Albany, N.Y.: State University of New York Press, 1994.

CHISHOLM, ANNE. *Philosophers of Earth*. New York: E. P. Dutton and Co., 1972.

COLE, RICHARD, OMI. *Re-Visioning Mission*. Mahwah, N.J.: Paulist Press, 1996.

COLLERAN, P.K., ed. *Walking with Contemplation*. Berkeley: Catholic Foundation, 1983.

CONLON, JAMES. *Earth Story, Sacred Story*. Mystic, Conn.: Twenty-Third Publications, 1994.

CONLON, JAMES. *Geo-Justice: A Preferential Option for the Earth*. San Jose, Calif.: Resource Publications, 1990.

CONLON, JAMES. *Lyrics for Re-Creation: Language for the Music of the Universe.* New York: Continuum, 1997.

CURRAN, CHARLES. *History and Contemporary Issues*. New York: Continuum, 1996.

DEAR, JOHN. *Apostle of Peace: Essays in Honor of Daniel Berrigan*. Maryknoll, N.Y.: Orbis Books, 1996.

DILLARD, ANNIE. *Holy the Firm*. San Francisco: Harper & Row, 1977.

DILLARD, ANNIE. *Teaching the Stone to Talk*. San Francisco: Harper & Row, 1977.

EDWARDS, DENNIS. *Jesus the Wisdom of God — An Ecological Theology*. Maryknoll, N.Y.: Orbis Books, 1995.

EISELEY, LOREN. *The Night Country*. Lincoln: University of Nebraska Press, 1997.

ERLICH, GRETEL. *The Solace of Open Spaces*. New York: Penguin Books, 1985.

FINKS, P. DAVID. *The Radical Vision of Saul Alinsky*. Mahwah, N.J.: Paulist Press, 1984.

FOWLER, JAMES. *Weaving the New Creation*. San Francisco: Harper, 1991.

FOX, MATTHEW. *Meditations with Meister Eckhart*. Santa Fe: Bear & Co., 1982.

FOX, WARWICH. *Toward a Transpersonal Ecology*. Boston: Shambala, 1992.

FRAGOMENI, RICHARD AND JOHN PAWLIKOWSKI, ed. *The Ecological Challenge*. Collegeville, Minn.: Liturgical Press, 1994.

FREIRE, PAULO. "Seminar on Community Education and Development." Toronto: Institute for Studies in Education, University of Toronto, 1976.

FREIRE, PAULO. *Education for Critical Consciousness*. New York: Seabury Press, 1973.

FREIRE, PAULO. *Pedagogy of Hope: Reliving the Pedagogy of the Oppressed*. New York: Continuum, 1989.

FREIRE, PAULO. *Pedagogy of the City*. New York: Continuum, 1993.

FREIRE, PAULO. *Pedagogy of the Oppressed*. New York: Seabury Press, 1970.

FREIRE, PAULO. *Teachers as Cultural Workers: Letters to Those Who Dare to Teach*. Boulder, Colo.: Westview Press, 1998.

FRITZ, ROBERT. *The Path of Least Resistance*. New York: Fawcett Columbine, 1989.

GAILLOT, BISHOP JACQUES. *Voice from the Desert*. New York: Crossroad, 1996.

GLOBAL EDUCATION ASSOCIATION. *Earth Covenant/Earth Charter: Ecological Wisdom and Action for the Twenty-First Century*. New York: Global Education Associates, 1996.

GORE, AL. *Earth in the Balance*. New York: Houghton Mifflin, 1992.

GRANBERG, WESLEY. *Redeeming the Creation — The Rio Earth Summit*. Michaelson-Risk Book Series, Geneva: World Council of Churches Publications, 1992.

GREEN, LORNA. *Earth Age — A New Vision of God, the Human and the Earth*. Mahwah, N.J.: Paulist Press, 1994.

GRIFFIN, SUSAN. *The Eros of Everyday Life*. New York: Anchor Books, 1995.

GRIFFITHS, BEDE. *A New Vision of Reality*. Springfield, Ill.: Templegate, 1989.

GROF, STANISLAV, WITH HAL BENNETT. *The Holotropic Mind*. San Francisco: Harper, 1990.

GUTIÉRREZ, GUSTAVO. *Sharing the World Through This Liturgical Year*. Maryknoll, N.Y.: Orbis Books, 1997.

GUTIÉRREZ, GUSTAVO. *The Theology of Liberation*. Maryknoll, N.Y.: Orbis Books, 1988.

GUTIÉRREZ, GUSTAVO. *We Drink from Our Own Wells*. Maryknoll, N.Y.: Orbis Books, 1984.

HALLMAN, DAVID, ed. *Voices from South and North*. Geneva: World Council of Churches Publications, and Maryknoll, N.Y.: Orbis Books, 1994.

HÄRING, BERNARD. *Priesthood Imperiled*. Liguori, Mo.: Triumph Books, 1996.

HARTE, JOHN. *The Green Fuse — An Ecological Odyssey*. Berkeley: University of California Press, 1993.

HAUGHT, JOHN. *The Promise of Nature: Ecology and Cosmic Purpose*. Mahwah, N.J.: Paulist Press, 1995.

HAYDEN, TOM, ed. *Irish Hunger.* Boulder, Colo.: Roberts Reinhart, 1997.

HAYDEN, TOM. *Lost Gospel of the Earth: A Call for Renewing Nature, Spirit and Politics.* San Francisco: Sierra Club Books, 1996.

HAYS, EDWARD. *Prayers for a Planetary Pilgrim*. Leavenworth, Kan.: Forest of Peace Publishing, 1989.

HAYS, EDWARD. *The Gospel of Gabriel*. Leavenworth, Kan.: Forest of Peace Publishing, 1996.

HAYS, EDWARD. *The Old Hermit's Almanac*. Leavenworth, Kan.: Forest of Peace Publishing, 1997.

HEFFERN, RICH. *Adventures in Simple Living*. New York: Crossroad, 1994.

HEFFERN, RICH. *Daybreak Within: Living in a Sacred World*. Leavenworth, Kan.: Forest of Peace Publishing, 1998.

HENNELLY, ALFRED T., S.J., ed. *Santa Domingo and Beyond: Documents and Commentaries from the Historic Meeting of the Latin American Bishops Conference*. Maryknoll, N.Y.: Orbis Books, 1993.

HESSEL, DIETER, ed. *After Nature's Revolt: Eco-Justice and Theology*. Minneapolis: Fortress Press, 1992.

HEYNEMAN, MARTHA. *The Breathing Cathedral*. San Francisco: Sierra Club Books, 1993.

HINDLEY-SMITH, LEA. *Secret Places*. Book 1 of La Covenir: A Trilogy from the Summonsa Tapestries. Toronto: A Therafields Book, 1976.

HORTON, MYLES, AND PAULO FREIRE. *We Make the Road by Walking*. Philadelphia: Temple University Press, 1990.

HORWITT, SANFORD. *Let Them Call Me Rebel*. New York: Alfred Knopf, 1989.

INGRAM, CATHERINE. *In the Footsteps of Ghandi*. Berkeley: Parallax Press, 1990.

JANTSCH, ERICH. *The Self-Organizing Universe: Scientific and Human Implications of the Emerging Paradigm of Evolution*. New York: Pergaman Press, 1980.

JENSEN, DERRICK. *Listening to the Land: Conversations about Nature, Culture, and Eros*. San Francisco: Sierra Club Books, 1995.

JOHNSON, ELIZABETH. *She Who Is*. New York: Crossroad, 1995.

KEEN, SAM. *Hymns to an Unknown God*. New York: Bantam Books, 1994.

KELLY, PETRA. *Thinking Green*. Berkeley, Calif.: Parallax Press, 1994.

KELLY, TONY. *An Expanding Theology*. Newton, NSW, Australia: E.J. Owyer, 1993.

KILLEN, PATRICIA O'CONNOR, AND JOHN DEBEER. *The Art of Theological Reflection*. New York: Crossroad, 1997.

KING, MARTIN LUTHER, JR. *I Have a Dream*. San Francisco: Harper, 1993.

KING, URSULA. *Christ in All Things: Exploring Spirituality with Teilhard de Chardin*. Maryknoll, N.Y.: Orbis Books, 1997.

KUHNS, WILLIAM. *The Post-Industrial Prophets*. New York: Waybright and Talley, 1971.

KOLBENSCHLAG, MADONNA. *Eastward Toward Eve: A Geography of Soul*. New York: Crossroad, 1996.

KRIPPNER, STANLEY, AND DAVID FEINSTEIN. *Personal Mythology: The Psychology of Your Evolving Self*. Los Angeles: Jeremy Tarcher, 1988.

LACHANCE, ALBERT, AND JOHN CARROLL, eds. *Embracing Earth — Catholic Approaches to Ecology*. Maryknoll, N.Y.: Orbis Books, 1994.

LARSON, JEAN, AND MADGE AND MICHAEL CYRUS. *Seeds of Peace*. Santa Cruz, Calif.: New Society Publishers, 1987.

LEECH, KENNETH. *The Eye of the Storm — Living Spiritually in the Real World*. San Francisco: Harper, 1982.

LEOPOLD, ALDO. *A Sand Country Almanac*. New York: Ballantine Books, 1966.

LINFIELD, MICHAEL. *The Dance of Change: An Eco-Spiritual Approach to Transformation*. New York: Routledge & Kegan Paul, 1986.

LOPEZ, BARRY. *Field Notes*. New York: Avon Books, 1994.

LOURDE, ANDRE. *Sister Outsider: Essays and Speeches*. Trumansburg, N.Y.: Crossing Press, 1984.

MACKINNOR, MARY HEATHER, AND MONI MCINTYRE, eds. *Readings in Ecology and Feminist Theology*. Kansas City: Sheed and Ward, 1995.

MANTIN-BARO, IGNACIO. *Writings for a Liberation Psychology*. Edited by Adrianne Aron and Shawn Corwe. Cambridge, Mass.: Harvard University Press, 1994.

MAY, ROLLO. *My Quest for Beauty*. New York: Saybrook Publishing Co., 1985.

MCBRIEN, RICHARD. *Catholicism*. Minneapolis: Winston Press, 1981.

MCDANIEL, JAY. *With Roots and Wings: Christianity in an Age of Ecology and Dialogue*. Maryknoll, N.Y.: Orbis Books, 1995.

MCDONAGH, SEAN. *Passion for the Earth*. Maryknoll, N.Y.: Orbis Books, 1995.

MCFAGUE, SALLIE. *Super, Natural Christians*. Minneapolis: Fortress Press, 1997.

MCKIBBON, BILL. *The End of Nature*. New York: Avon Books, 1989.

MERCHANT, CAROLYN, ed. *Ecology*. Atlantic Highlands, N.J.: Humanities Press, 1994.

MERCHANT, CAROLYN. *Radical Ecology — The Search for a Liveable World*. New York/London: Routledge, 1992.

MERTON, THOMAS. *Conjectures of a Guilty Bystander*. Garden City, N.Y.: Doubleday and Co., 1966.

MERTON, THOMAS. *Contemplation in a World of Action*. London, Boston, Sydney: Mandala Books, Unwin Paperbacks, 1980.

MERTON, THOMAS. *Preview of the Asian Journey*. Ed. William Capps. New York: Crossroad, 1989.

MILLER, GORDON. *Wisdom of the Earth: Visions of an Ecological Faith*. Seattle: Green Rock Press, 1997.

MILLER, RONALD, and editors of *New Age Journal*. *As Above So Below*. Los Angeles: Jeremy Tarcher, 1992.

MOORE, THOMAS. *Soul Mates*. New York: HarperCollins, 1994.

NICKOLOFF, JAMES, ed. *Gustavo Gutiérrez — Essential Writings*. Minneapolis: Fortress Press, 1996.

NOLAN, ALBERT. *God in South Africa*. Grand Rapids, Mich.: Eerdmann, 1988.

NORTHCOTT, MICHAEL. *The Environment and Christian Ethics*. New York: Cambridge University Press, 1996.

O'DONOHUE, JOHN. *Aman Cara: A Book of Celtic Wisdom.* New York: HarperCollins, 1997.

OKULAM, FRODO. *The Julian Mystique.* Mystic, Conn.: Twenty-Third Publications, 1994.

OLIVA, MAX. *The Masculine Spirit: Resources for Reflective Living.* Notre Dame, Ind.: Ave Maria Press, 1997.

OLIVER, MARY. *New and Selected Poems.* Boston: Beacon Press, 1992.

O'MEARA, THOMAS. *Thomas Aquinas: Theologian.* Notre Dame, Ind.: University of Notre Dame, 1997.

O'MURCHU, DIARMUID. *Quantum Theology: Spiritual Implications of the New Physics.* New York: Crossroad, 1997.

PALMER, PARKER. *The Courage to Teach: Exploring the Inner Landscape of a Teacher's Life.* San Francisco: Jersey-Bass Publishers, 1997.

PATRICK, ANNE. *Liberating Conscience.* New York: Continuum, 1996.

PETERS, TED. *For the Love of Children.* Louisville, Ky.: Westminster/John Knox Press, 1996.

PIERIS, ALOYSIUS, S.J. *An Asian Theology of Liberation.* Maryknoll, N.Y.: Orbis Books, 1988.

PURPLE, DAVID. *The Moral and Spiritual Crisis in Education.* New York: Bergen & Garvey, 1989.

QUOIST, MICHEL. *Prayers.* New York: Sheed & Ward, 1963.

RAE, ELEANOR. *Women, the Earth, the Divine.* Maryknoll, N.Y.: Orbis Books, 1994.

RASSMUSSEN, LARRY. *Earth Community, Earth Ethics.* Maryknoll, N.Y.: Orbis Books, 1994.

REICH, WILHELM. *The Murder of Christ.* New York: Noonday Press, 1970.

ROCKEFELLER, STEPHEN, ed. *Spirit and Nature.* Boston: Beacon Press, 1992.

RODGERS, MARY BETH. *Cold Anger.* Denton, Tex.: University of North Texas Press, 1990.

ROSZAK, T., M. GOMES, A. KANNER, eds. *Eco Psychology: Restoring the Earth — Healing the Mind.* San Francisco: Sierra Club Books, 1995.

ROSZAK, THEODORE. *The Voice of the Earth.* New York: Simon & Schuster, 1992.

RUETHER, ROSEMARY RADFORD. *Gaia and God: An Ecofeminist Theology of Earth Healing.* San Francisco: HarperCollins, 1992..

RUETHER, ROSEMARY RADFORD. *New Woman, New Earth.* New York: Seabury Press, 1974.

RUETHER, ROSEMARY RADFORD. *Sexism and God-Talk.* Boston: Beacon, 1983.

RUETHER, ROSEMARY RADFORD. *Women Guides: Readings Toward a Feminist Theology*. Boston: Beacon, 1988 (reprinted 1996).

RUETHER, ROSEMARY RADFORD. *Women Healing Earth*. Boston: Beacon, 1996.

SCHAEF, ANNE WILSON. *Beyond Therapy*. San Francisco: Harper, 1992.

SCHARPER, STEPHEN. *The Redeeming Time: A Political Theology of the Environment*. New York: Continuum, 1997.

SCHUMACHER, E. F. *A Guide for the Perplexed*. San Francisco: Harper & Row, 1977.

SESSIONS, GEORGE, ed. *Deep Ecology for the 21st Century*. Boston: Shambala, 1995.

SEITZ, RON. *Song for Nobody: The Memory Vision of Thomas Merton*. Ligouri, Mo.: Ligouri Press, 1993.

SHANNON, WILLIAM, ed. *Passion for Peace: The Social Essays of Thomas Merton*. New York: Crossroad, 1995.

SHEA, JOHN. *Gospel Light: Jesus Stories for Spiritual Consciousness*. New York: Crossroad, 1998.

SHEA, JOHN. *Starlight*. New York: Crossroad, 1995.

SIMPKINSON, CHARLES, AND ANNE SIMPKINSON, eds. *Sacred Stories — A Celebration of the Power of Stories to Transform and Heal*. San Francisco: HarperCollins, 1993.

SKOLIMOWSKI, HENDRYK. *A Sacred Place to Dwell: Living with Reverence Upon the Earth*. Rockport, Mass.: Element, Inc., 1993.

SMITH, MCGREGOR, JR. *Now That You Know: A Journey Toward Earth Literacy*. Washburn, Tenn.: Earth Knows Publications, 1997.

SOELLE, DOROTHEE. *On Earth As in Heaven*. Louisville: John Knox Press, 1993.

SOELLE, DOROTHEE. *Theology for Skeptics — Reflections on God*. Minneapolis: Fortress Press, 1995.

STEINDL-RAST, DAVID, OSB. *The Music of Silence*. San Francisco/New York: Harper, 1995.

SWIMME, BRIAN. *The Universe Is a Green Dragon*. Santa Fe, N.M.: Bear & Co., 1984.

SWIMME, BRIAN. *Hidden Heart of the Cosmos*. Maryknoll, N.Y.: Orbis Books, 1996.

TARDIFF, MARY, O.P., ed. *At Home in the World: The Letters of Thomas Merton and Rosemary Radford Ruether*. Maryknoll, N.Y.: Orbis Books, 1995.

TARNAS, RICHARD. *The Passion of the Western Mind: Understanding the Ideas That Have Shaped Our World View*. New York: Ballantine Books, 1991.

TEILHARD DE CHARDIN, PIERRE. *The Divine Milieu*. New York: Harper & Row, 1960.

TEILHARD DE CHARDIN, PIERRE. *The Heart of Matter*. New York: Harcourt Brace, 1978.

THICH NHAT HANH. *Being Peace*. Berkeley, Calif.: Parallax Press, 1981.

THOMPSON, WILLIAM ERWIN. *Darkness and Shattered Light*. Garden City, N.Y.: Anchor-Doubleday, 1978.

TICKLE, PHYLLIS. *God-Talk in America*. New York: Crossroad, 1997.

TILBY, ANGELA. *Science and the Soul*. London: SPCK, 1992.

TILLEY, TERRENCE. *Postmodern Theology: The Challenge of Religious Diversity*. Maryknoll, N.Y.: Orbis Books, 1995.

TOBIAS, MICHAEL AND GEORGIANNE COWAN. *The Soul of Nature — Visions of a Living Earth*. New York: Continuum, 1994.

TOUAR, BRIAN. *The Green Alternative — Creating an Ecological Future*. R.E. Miles, PO Box 1916, San Pedro, Calif. 90733.

TUCKER, MARY EVELYN AND JOHN GRIM, eds. *World Views and Ecology: Religion, Philosophy and the Environment*. Maryknoll, N.Y.: Orbis Books, 1994.

WAGONER, DAVID. *Lost in the Forgotten Language: Contemporary Poets and Nature*. Ed. Christopher Morrill. Layton, Utah: Peregrine Smith Books, 1991.

WALLIS, JIM. *The Soul of Politics*. New York: The New Press, and Maryknoll, N.Y.: Orbis Books, 1994.

WALSH, NEAL DONALD. *Conversations with God*. New York: Putnam & Sons, 1996.

WALSHE, PETER. *Prophetic Christianity and the Liberation Movement in South Africa*. Pietermarrburg, South Africa: Cluster Publications, 1995.

WHEATLEY, MARGARET. *Leadership and the New Science*. San Francisco: Barnett-Koehler Publications, 1992.

WHYTE, DAVID. *The House of Belonging*. Langley, Wash.: Many Rivers Press, 1997.

WILDER, AMOS NIVEN. *Theopoetic: Theology and the Religious Imagination*. Philadelphia: Fortress Press, 1976.

WINTER, GIBSON. *America in Search of Its Soul*. Harrisburg, Pa.: Morehouse Publishing, 1996.

ZOHAR, DANAH, AND IAN MARSHALL. *The Quantum Society: Mind, Physics and a New Social Vision*. New York: William Morrow & Co., 1994.